# Math Skills

## Grade 5

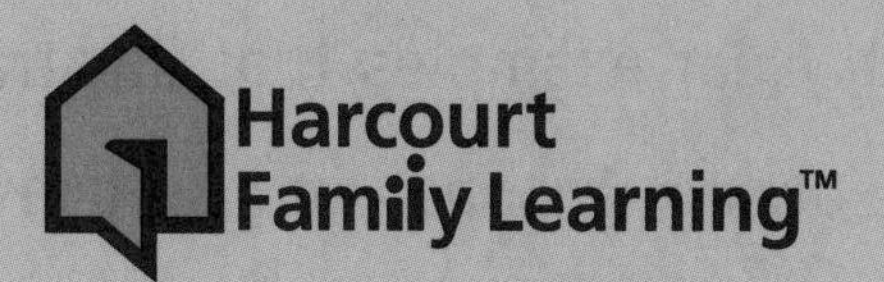



Adapted from *Steck-Vaughn Working with Numbers, Level E*


Illustrator: Janee Trasler



ISBN: 978-1-4114-0110-5

Please submit all inquiries to FlashKids@bn.com

Printed and bound in Canada

Lot#:

26 25

06/14

**Flash Kids**
A Division of Barnes & Noble
122 Fifth Avenue
New York, NY 10011

## Dear Parent,

As you bring math learning into the home, you are helping your child to strengthen the skills that he or she is taught in the classroom. Your efforts also emphasize how math is useful outside of school, as well as necessary for success in everyday life.

To assist you, this colorful, fun workbook presents grade-appropriate math concepts and language to your child in a way that is logical and organized. Each section begins with clear examples that illustrate new skills, and then practice drills, problem-solving lessons, and unit reviews encourage your child to master each new technique.

This Grade 5–level workbook begins with exercises that refresh your child's ability to calculate sums and differences. Then Units 2 and 3 reinforce techniques for solving complex multiplication and division problems. Building on the basic understanding of fractions learned in Grade 4, here Unit 4 teaches the addition and subtraction of both simple and complex fractions. Next, decimals are introduced in Unit 5, including skills for comparing, estimating, adding, and subtracting decimals. Lastly, Units 6 and 7 further develop your child's grasp of customary and metric units of measure, as well as geometric concepts such as area and perimeter.

As you and your child work through each unit, try to show your child how to apply each skill in everyday situations. For example, you can ask your child to calculate how many quarts of milk you need to buy for the week, if each family member will drink two eight-ounce glasses a day, and you still need 2 cups left over to use in a recipe later in the week. This exercise requires your child to apply many different math skills to a single, real-life problem. As your child draws connections between concepts presented separately in this workbook, he or she learns to reason mathematically, an ability critical for success through future years of math instruction.

Also, consider how you can turn the following activities into fun math exercises for you and your child to do together:

- Comparing distances between towns and other sites during car trips;
- Purchasing enough food and drinks for a family dinner or a party;
- Estimating the proper tip for a restaurant bill;
- Calculating how much material is needed to make new curtains, build bookshelves, or carpet a room;
- Determining how much time is left before the next planned activity of the day;
- Measuring ingredients to be used in cooking, and, if necessary, dividing amounts to adjust the recipe.

Use your imagination! With help from you and this workbook, your child is well on the way to math proficiency.

# Table of Contents

## unit 1

## unit 2

## unit 3

## unit 4

## unit 5

### Decimals



## unit 6

### Measurement



## unit 7

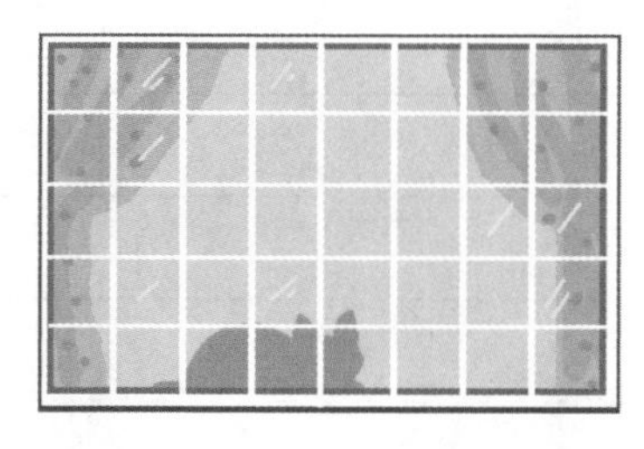

### Geometry

# unit 1
## whole numbers

### Place Value

A **place-value chart** can help you understand **whole numbers**.
Each **digit** in a number has a value based on its place in the number.

The 7 is in the millions place.
Its value is 7 millions or 7,000,000.
The 5 is in the ten-thousands place.
Its value is 5 ten thousands or 50,000.
The 3 is in the hundreds place.
Its value is 3 hundreds or 300.

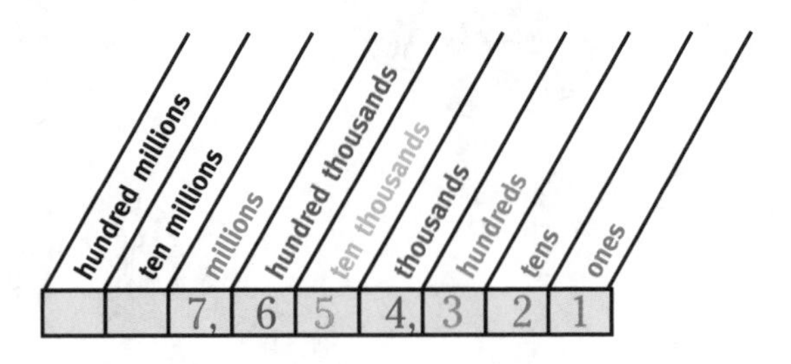


**Write each number in the place-value chart.**

1. 366,789,302
2. 2,304,361
3. 19,076,541
4. 8,854,632
5. 97,065
6. 8,005,002

| | hundred millions | ten millions | millions | hundred thousands | ten thousands | thousands | hundreds | tens | ones |
|---|---|---|---|---|---|---|---|---|---|
| 1. | 3 | 6 | 6, | 7 | 8 | 9, | 3 | 0 | 2 |
| 2. | | | | | | | | | |
| 3. | | | | | | | | | |
| 4. | | | | | | | | | |
| 5. | | | | | | | | | |
| 6. | | | | | | | | | |

**Write the place name for the 5 in each number.**

| | a | | b |
|---|---|---|---|
| 7. | 362,050 ___tens___ | | 2,250,876 ______ |
| 8. | 219,572,080 ______ | | 5,712,309 ______ |
| 9. | 876,529 ______ | | 1,804,075 ______ |
| 10. | 15,782 ______ | | 53,047,260 ______ |

**Write the value of the underlined digit.**

| | a | | b |
|---|---|---|---|
| 11. | 1,39<u>0</u>,526 ___0 thousands___ | | 207,3<u>8</u>9 ______ |
| 12. | 9<u>8</u>3,576,091 ______ | | <u>4</u>,523,551 ______ |
| 13. | <u>4</u>50,086 ______ | | 232,87<u>5</u> ______ |
| 14. | <u>1</u>72,034,056 ______ | | 67,<u>0</u>43 ______ |

## Reading and Writing Numbers

Comiskey Park and Wrigley Field are baseball stadiums in Chicago. The two stadiums together hold about 81,960 people.

We read and write this number as:
eighty-one thousand, nine hundred sixty.

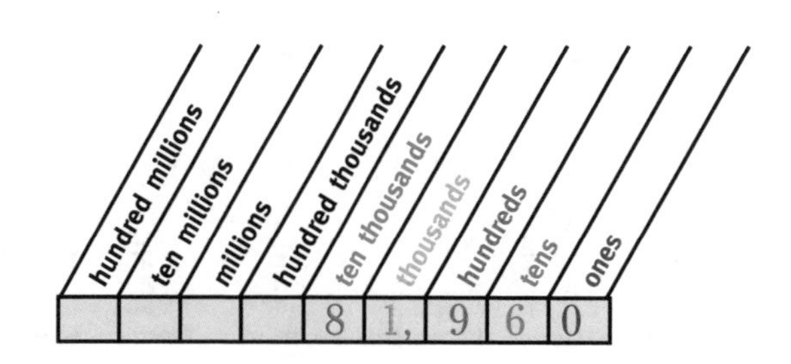


The digit 8 means 8 ten thousands, or 80,000.
The digit 1 means 1 thousand, or 1,000.
The digit 9 means 9 hundreds, or 900.
The digit 6 means 6 tens, or 60.
The digit 0 means 0 ones, or 0.

Notice that commas are used to separate the digits into groups of three called **periods**. This helps make larger numbers easier to read.

**Rewrite each number. Insert commas where needed.**

| | a | b | c |
|---|---|---|---|
| **1.** | 758493 *758,493* | 6473829 ______ | 868582 ______ |
| **2.** | 2030200 ______ | 5000400 ______ | 6050407 ______ |
| **3.** | 30782 ______ | 406702 ______ | 3908454 ______ |

**Write each number using digits. Insert commas where needed.**

**4.** seven hundred twenty thousand, four hundred sixty-two *720,462*

**5.** twenty-five thousand, two hundred one ______

**6.** one hundred eighty-four thousand, thirty-nine ______

**7.** one hundred million, two hundred forty-three thousand ______

**Write each number in words. Insert commas where needed.**

**8.** 16,349 *sixteen thousand, three hundred forty-nine*

**9.** 776 ______

**10.** 123,456 ______

# Addition

To add, start with the digits in the ones place. **Regroup** as needed.

**Find: 796 + 304**

Add the ones. Regroup.

| | Th | H | T | O |
|---|---|---|---|---|
| | | | 1 | |
| | | 7 | 9 | 6 |
| + | | 3 | 0 | 4 |
| | | | | 0 |

Add the tens. Regroup.

| | Th | H | T | O |
|---|---|---|---|---|
| | | 1 | 1 | |
| | | 7 | 9 | 6 |
| + | | 3 | 0 | 4 |
| | | | 0 | 0 |

Add the hundreds. Regroup.

| | Th | H | T | O |
|---|---|---|---|---|
| | 1 | 1 | 1 | |
| | | 7 | 9 | 6 |
| + | | 3 | 0 | 4 |
| | 1, | 1 | 0 | 0 |

**Add.**

**1.**
a. 450 + 394 = 844 (regrouped 1 in the hundreds place)
b. 251 + 366
c. 558 + 645
d. 712 + 678

**2.**
a. 394 + 759
b. 654 + 506
c. 431 + 687
d. 750 + 947

**3.**
a. 639 + 82
b. 46 + 567
c. 826 + 79
d. 35 + 806

**4.**
a. 97 + 344
b. 532 + 19
c. 605 + 56
d. 493 + 28

**Add.**

| | a | b | c | d | e |
|---|---|---|---|---|---|
| **5.** | 5,646<br>+2,387 | 4,483<br>+1,930 | 2,557<br>+4,963 | 2,904<br>+6,325 | 1,663<br>+ 975 |
| **6.** | 521<br>+9,031 | 7,662<br>+1,517 | 8,605<br>+ 87 | 6,554<br>+2,671 | 863<br>+7,506 |
| **7.** | 5,211<br>+3,687 | 3,051<br>+5,289 | 6,584<br>+ 620 | 999<br>+1,111 | 6,513<br>+2,976 |

**Line up the digits. Then find the sums.**

| | a | b | c |
|---|---|---|---|
| **8.** | 3,697 + 840 = ________<br>3,697<br>+ 840 | 4,305 + 5,224 = ________ | 7,981 + 375 = ________ |
| **9.** | 5,208 + 3,114 = ________ | 8,372 + 609 = ________ | 2,584 + 2,639 = ________ |

## Problem-Solving Method: Make a Graph

Carlos has a meeting with his boss next week. He wants to show her that sales have increased since he became manager of the store in January. What would be a good way for him to present the sales data in this table?

| Month | Jan. | Feb. | Mar. | Apr. | May | June |
|---|---|---|---|---|---|---|
| TVs Sold | 27 | 32 | 29 | 30 | 35 | 40 |

**Understand the problem.**

- **What do you want to know?**
  a good way to present the sales data

- **What information is given?**
  the sales from January to June

**Plan how to solve it.**

- **What method can you use?**
  You can make a line graph to show how the sales have increased over time.

**Solve it.**

- **How can you use this method to solve the problem?**
  Make a graph with the months listed along the bottom and the sales along the side. Make a dot where each month meets its sales number. Then connect the dots with a line.

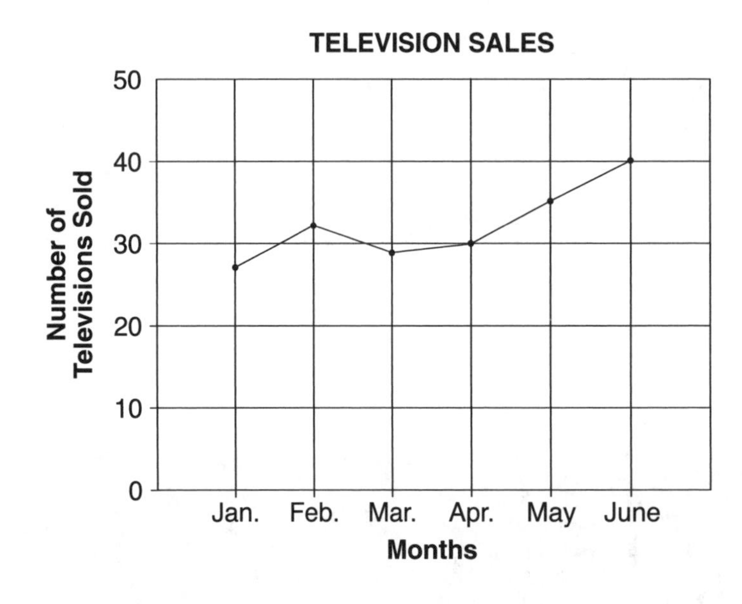


- **What is the answer?**
  A line graph is a good way to display the data.

**Look back and check your answer.**

- **Is your answer reasonable?**
  Since the line on the graph slants up and to the right, it shows that sales are increasing.

  The answer is reasonable.

**Make a line graph to display the data in each table.**

**1.** **Games Won by Houston Astros**

| Year | 1995 | 1996 | 1997 | 1998 | 1999 |
|---|---|---|---|---|---|
| Wins | 76 | 82 | 84 | 102 | 97 |

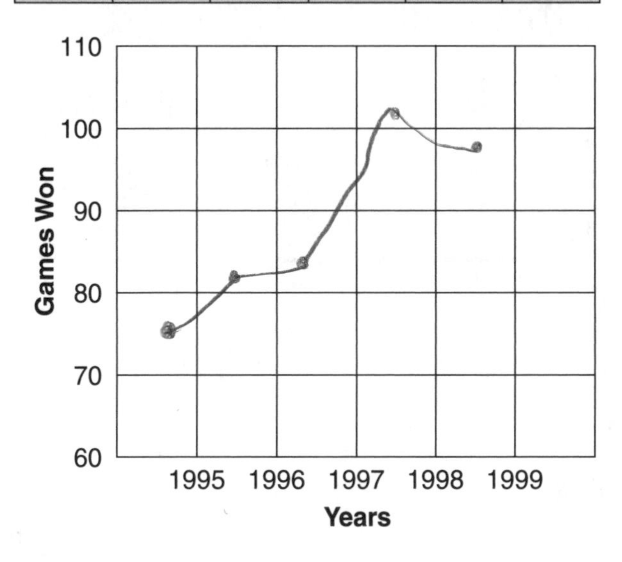


**2.** **Average Temperature Rapid City, South Dakota**

| Month | Apr. | May | June | July | Aug. |
|---|---|---|---|---|---|
| Temp. | 45° | 55° | 65° | 72° | 71° |

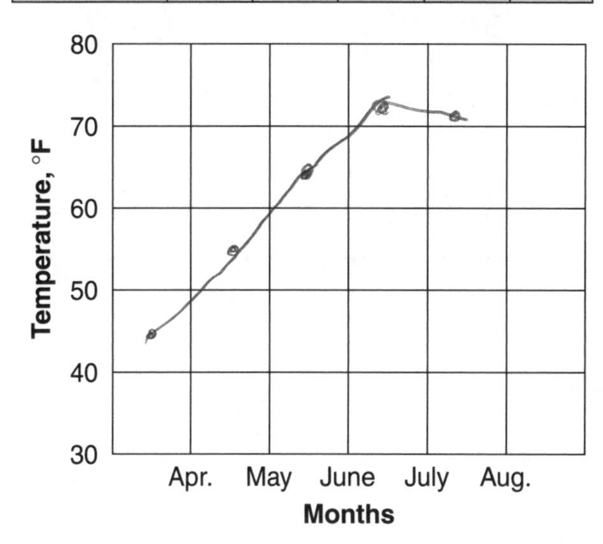

# Addition of Three or More Numbers

To add three or more numbers, use the same steps as when adding two numbers.

**Find: 949 + 753 + 531**

Add the ones. Regroup.

| | Th | H | T | O |
|---|---|---|---|---|
| | | | 1 | |
| | | 9 | 4 | 9 |
| | | 7 | 5 | 3 |
| + | | 5 | 3 | 1 |
| | | | | 3 |

Add the tens. Regroup.

| | Th | H | T | O |
|---|---|---|---|---|
| | | 1 | 1 | |
| | | 9 | 4 | 9 |
| | | 7 | 5 | 3 |
| + | | 5 | 3 | 1 |
| | | | 3 | 3 |

Add the hundreds. Regroup.

| | Th | H | T | O |
|---|---|---|---|---|
| | 2 | 1 | 1 | |
| | | 9 | 4 | 9 |
| | | 7 | 5 | 3 |
| + | | 5 | 3 | 1 |
| | 2, | 2 | 3 | 3 |

**Add.**

| | a | b | c | d | e |
|---|---|---|---|---|---|
| **1.** | 1 2<br>256<br>249<br>+157<br>662 | 419<br>617<br>+314 | 98<br>106<br>+307 | 25<br>90<br>+208 | 105<br>62<br>+ 7 |
| **2.** | 213<br>117<br>234<br>+525 | 559<br>304<br>205<br>+198 | 438<br>160<br>638<br>+106 | 718<br>164<br>130<br>+607 | 265<br>322<br>674<br>+439 |

**Line up the digits. Then find the sums.**

a

**3.** 149 + 753 + 531 = ______________

149
753
+531

b

489 + 189 + 78 = ______________

# Subtraction

To subtract, start with the digits in the ones place. Regroup as needed.

**Find: 836 – 449**

| Subtract the ones. Regroup. | Subtract the tens. Regroup. | Subtract the hundreds. |
|---|---|---|
| H T O | H T O | H T O |
| | 12 | 12 |
| 2 16 | 7 ~~2~~ 16 | 7 ~~2~~ 16 |
| 8 ~~3~~ ~~6~~ | ~~8~~ ~~3~~ ~~6~~ | ~~8~~ ~~3~~ ~~6~~ |
| − 4 4 9 | − 4 4 9 | − 4 4 9 |
| 7 | 8 7 | 3 8 7 |

**Subtract.**

| | a | b | c | d |
|---|---|---|---|---|
| **1.** | H T O<br>12<br>7 ~~2~~ 13<br>~~8~~ ~~3~~ ~~3~~<br>− 2 8 7<br>5 4 6 | H T O<br>6 9 2<br>− 1 1 8 | H T O<br>5 9 2<br>− 3 4 5 | H T O<br>6 9 1<br>− 2 8 8 |
| **2.** | H T O<br>8 4 7<br>− 1 3 8 | H T O<br>9 6 8<br>− 6 5 9 | H T O<br>9 7 6<br>− 6 1 7 | H T O<br>9 3 2<br>− 8 2 9 |
| **3.** | H T O<br>2 0 0<br>− 3 5 | H T O<br>4 9 3<br>− 6 2 | H T O<br>9 0 6<br>− 3 2 | H T O<br>3 1 8<br>− 6 6 |
| **4.** | H T O<br>9 7 4<br>− 8 8 5 | H T O<br>6 1 2<br>− 5 1 3 | H T O<br>7 7 1<br>− 3 4 9 | H T O<br>5 6 0<br>− 9 1 |

Subtract.

| | a | b | c | d | e |
|---|---|---|---|---|---|
| **5.** | 5,646<br>−2,387 | 4,483<br>−1,930 | 2,557<br>− 963 | 2,904<br>−1,325 | 1,663<br>− 975 |
| **6.** | 5,521<br>−2,031 | 7,662<br>−1,517 | 8,605<br>− 87 | 6,554<br>−2,671 | 4,863<br>−3,506 |
| **7.** | 5,211<br>−3,687 | 8,051<br>−5,289 | 6,584<br>− 620 | 1,111<br>− 999 | 6,513<br>−2,976 |

**Line up the digits. Then find the differences.**

| | a | b | c |
|---|---|---|---|
| **8.** | 3,697 − 840 = ________<br>3,697<br>− 840 | 5,305 − 4,224 = ________ | 7,981 − 375 = ________ |
| **9.** | 5,208 − 3,114 = ________ | 8,372 − 609 = ________ | 3,584 − 2,639 = ________ |

## Addition and Subtraction of Larger Numbers

To add or subtract larger numbers, start with the ones digits.
Regroup as needed.

**Add.**

| | a | b | c | d |
|---|---|---|---|---|
| **1.** | 1 1 1 1<br>38,917<br>+61,197<br>100,114 | 56,459<br>+46,554 | 67,943<br>+90,498 | 6,758<br>+63,284 |
| **2.** | 19,789<br>+ 219 | 94,387<br>+ 589 | 17,000<br>+ 2,000 | 18,554<br>+ 446 |

**Subtract.**

| | a | b | c | d |
|---|---|---|---|---|
| **3.** | 15 12 11<br>3 5 2 1 15<br>46,325<br>−17,858<br>28,467 | 56,452<br>−27,564 | 45,384<br>−17,596 | 63,338<br>−27,949 |
| **4.** | 70,903<br>− 5,994 | 30,000<br>− 4,000 | 53,326<br>− 947 | 67,334<br>− 3,558 |

**Line up the digits. Then add or subtract.**

| | a | b |
|---|---|---|
| **5.** | 27,002 − 13,849 = ______________<br>27,002<br>−13,849 | 62,525 + 13,475 = ______________ |

# Estimation of Sums and Differences

To **estimate** a sum or difference, first **round** each number to the same place value. Then add or subtract the rounded numbers.

**Estimate: 765 + 321**

Round each number to the same place value. Add.

| | |
|---|---|
| 765 → | 800 |
| +321 → | + 300 |
| | 1,100 |

**Estimate: 2,694 − 743**

Round each number to the same place value. Subtract.

| | |
|---|---|
| 2,694 → | 2,700 |
| − 743 → | − 700 |
| | 2,000 |

**Estimate the sums.**

| | a | b | c | d |
|---|---|---|---|---|
| 1. | 248 → 200<br>+381 → +400<br>600 | 264 → 300<br>+395 → 400<br>700 | 293 → 300<br>+346 → 300<br>600 | 274 → 300<br>+242 → 200<br>500 |
| 2. | 638 → 600<br>+291 → 300<br>900 | 543 → 500<br>+376 → 400<br>900 | 254 → 300<br>+403 → 400<br>700 | 181 → 200<br>+475 → 500<br>700 |

**Estimate the differences.**

| | a | b | c | d |
|---|---|---|---|---|
| 3. | 911 → 900<br>−779 → −800<br>100 | 933 → 900<br>−426 → 400<br>500 | 622 → 600<br>−189 → 200<br>400 | 511 → 500<br>−134 → 100<br>400 |
| 4. | 1,199 → 1200<br>− 619 → 600<br>600 | 1,041 → 1000<br>− 717 → 700<br>300 | 1,491 → 1500<br>− 888 → 900<br>600 | 1,292 → 1300<br>− 418 → 400<br>900 |

**Estimate the sums or differences.**

| | *a* | *b* | *c* | *d* |
|---|---|---|---|---|
| **5.** | 2 7 5 → 200 <br> +3 2 6 → 300 <br> 600 | 4 2 1 → 400 <br> +1 6 4 → 200 <br> 600 | 8 4 7 → 800 <br> −1 2 5 → 100 <br> 700 | 5 0 9 → 500 <br> +3 8 7 → 400 <br> 900 |
| **6.** | 4 7 9 → 500 <br> −2 1 6 → 200 <br> 300 | 6 5 2 → 700 <br> −1 5 0 → 200 <br> 500 | 1 2 4 → 100 <br> +3 6 9 → 400 <br> 500 | 8 0 6 → 800 <br> +2 2 4 → 200 <br> 1000 |
| **7.** | 1,3 5 7 → 1400 <br> − 2 5 3 → 300 <br> 1100 | 6,5 4 3 → 6500 <br> + 3 1 6 → 300 <br> 6800 | 4,7 2 5 → 4700 <br> − 1 4 8 → 100 <br> 4600 | 5 6 3 → 600 <br> +3,7 8 2 → 3800 <br> 4400 |
| **8.** | 4 9 9 → 500 <br> +3,2 4 3 → 3200 <br> 3300 | 9,3 2 7 → 9300 <br> − 1 7 5 → 200 <br> 9100 | 7,6 0 4 → 7600 <br> − 5 9 3 → 600 <br> 7000 | 6,2 2 1 → 6200 <br> + 6 5 4 → 700 <br> 7100 |
| **9.** | 8,5 5 7 → 8600 <br> −2,8 0 6 → 2800 <br> 11400 | 3,2 1 5 → 3200 <br> +5,4 2 7 → 5400 <br> 8600 | 6,9 8 6 → 7000 <br> −5,7 9 5 → 5800 <br> 1200 | 4,0 9 8 → 4100 <br> +4,9 0 8 → 4900 <br> 9000 |

## Problem-Solving Method: Work Backwards

Ted has 125 baseball cards. Lucia has 130 baseball cards. Last week, Ted traded 12 cards to Lucia for 9 of her cards. How many cards did Lucia have before the trade?

**Understand the problem.**

- **What do you want to know?**
  how many cards Lucia had before the trade

- **What information is given?**
  Ted has 125 cards now and Lucia has 130 cards now.
  Ted gave 12 cards to Lucia.
  Lucia gave 9 cards to Ted.

**Plan how to solve it.**

- **What method can you use?**
  Since you know how many cards Lucia has now, you can work backwards to find how many she started with.

**Solve it.**

- **How can you use this method to solve the problem?**
  Addition and subtraction are opposite operations. So, add the cards she gave and subtract the cards she got.

| | |
|---|---|
| 130 | ← Lucia has 130 cards now. |
| − 12 | ← Ted gave her 12 cards. Subtract 12 cards. |
| 118 | |
| + 9 | ← Lucia gave 9 cards to Ted. Add back 9 cards. |
| 127 | |

- **What is the answer?**
  Before the trade, Lucia had 127 baseball cards.

**Look back and check your answer.**

- **Is your answer reasonable?**
  You can check by working forwards from the number of cards she had before the trade.

| | |
|---|---|
| 127 | ← Lucia had 127 cards. |
| − 9 | ← She gave 9 cards to Ted. |
| 118 | |
| + 12 | ← Ted gave Lucia 12 cards. |
| 130 | ← Lucia has 130 cards now. |

The number of cards she has now matches.
The answer is reasonable.

**1.** A farmer planted 86 acres of soybeans and 65 acres of corn. Last year, 20 of the acres now used for corn were used for soybeans. How many acres of corn did the farmer have last year?

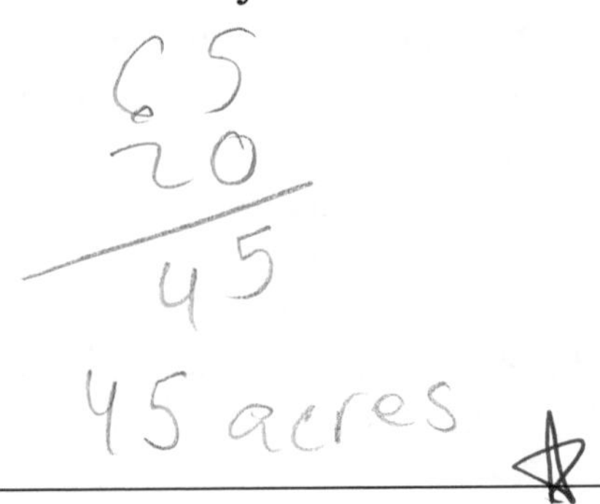

Answer ______________________

**2.** Jan spent $45 for two new shirts and $60 for a pair of jeans. She has $7 left over. How much money did Jan take shopping?

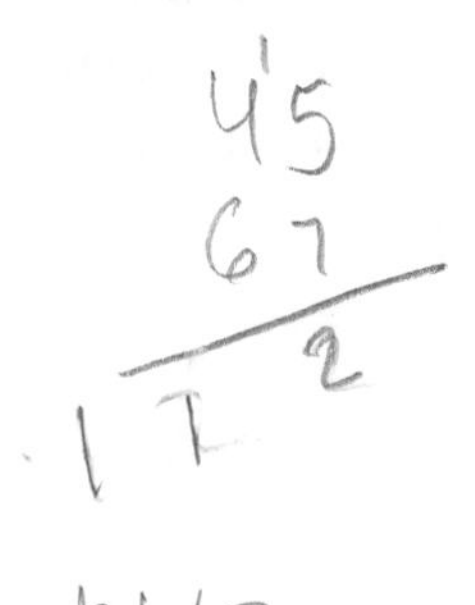

Answer ______________________

**3.** Shameeka sold her hamsters to a pet store. This doubled the number of hamsters in the store. Then the store got 6 more hamsters. If the pet store has 46 hamsters now, how many did Shameeka sell to the store?

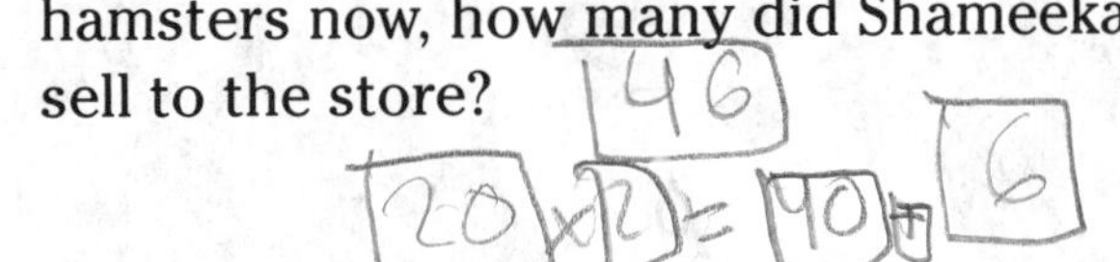

Answer ______________________

**4.** Wong's flight left at 7:00. It took him one and a half hours to check in at the airport. His house is an hour drive from the airport. At what time did Wong leave his house to get to the airport?

Answer ______________________

**5.** The club treasury ended the week with $76. On Friday, the treasurer had received $35 in club dues. On Tuesday, she had paid a bill of $15. How much money was in the treasury at the beginning of the week?

Answer ______________________

## Problem Solving

**Solve.**

**1.** At 3,212 feet, Angel Falls in Venezuela is the tallest waterfall in the world. Yosemite Falls in California is 2,425 feet tall. How much taller is Angel Falls than Yosemite Falls?

Answer 787 ft.

**2.** The United States, Britain, and Germany are top Nobel Prize–winning countries. If the U.S. won 241, Britain 98, and Germany 73, how many Nobel Prizes have the three countries won altogether?

Answer 412 Prizes

**3.** *Apollo 8* flew 550,000 miles on its trip around the moon. *Apollo 9* flew 3,700,000 miles. How far did the two *Apollo* missions fly altogether?

Answer 4,250,000

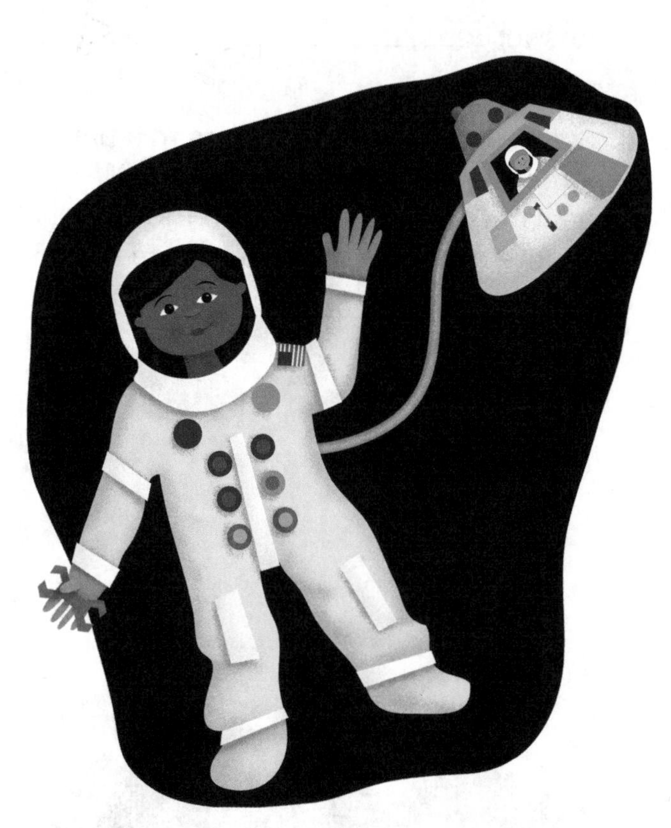

**4.** The area of North Carolina is 52,672 square miles. South Carolina covers 31,189 square miles. What is the combined area of the Carolinas?

Answer 83861 sq miles

**5.** Emily drove from Washington, D.C., to Boston, stopping once in New York. It is about 233 miles from Washington to New York and then about 206 miles from New York to Boston. Estimate how far Emily drove in all.

Answer 440 miles

**6.** In 2000, there were 854 endangered species of animals in the United States and 247 in Mexico. Estimate how many more endangered species there were in the U.S. than in Mexico.

Answer 600 more

# UNIT 1 Review

**Write the place name for the 4 in each number.**

| | a | b |
|---|---|---|
| **1.** | 3,470,981 ________ | 3,504,972 ________ |
| **2.** | 4,168,953 ________ | 1,040,831 ________ |
| **3.** | 8,031,142 ________ | 831,429 ________ |

**Write the value of the underlined digit.**

| | a | b |
|---|---|---|
| **4.** | $16,\underline{0}35$ ________ | $214,20\underline{3}$ ________ |
| **5.** | $\underline{9}68,137$ ________ | $13,641,2\underline{5}4$ ________ |
| **6.** | $\underline{6},899$ ________ | $\underline{1}34,618,349$ ________ |

**Write each number using digits. Insert commas where needed.**

**7.** seventy-two thousand, eighty-five ________

**8.** two million, forty thousand, five hundred six ________

**9.** seventeen million, five hundred thousand, eighteen ________

**Write each number in words. Insert commas where needed.**

**10.** 21,106 ________

**11.** 403,872 ________

**12.** 1,720,564 ________

**Add.**

| | a | b | c | d |
|---|---|---|---|---|
| **13.** | 428 + 229 | 167 + 92 | 405 + 540 + 764 | 112 + 485 + 368 |
| **14.** | 132 + 278 + 402 + 358 | 29,274 + 13,296 | 64,357 + 35,764 | 27,809 + 2,195 |

**Line up the digits. Then find the sums.**

**15.** a 449 + 223 + 720 = ______ b 8,629 + 6,587 = ______

**Subtract.**

| | a | b | c | d |
|---|---|---|---|---|
| **16.** | 53,647 − 28,658 | 37,853 − 7,865 | 62,503 − 47,123 | 64,971 − 14,921 |

**Line up the digits. Then find the differences.**

**17.** a 795 − 658 = ______ b 9,235 − 479 = ______

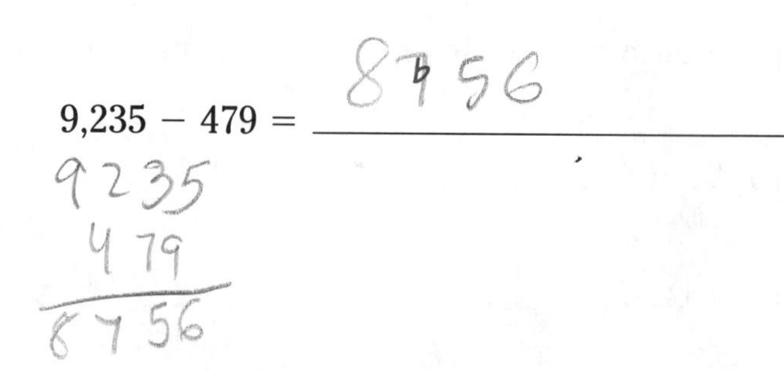

**Estimate the sums or differences.**

| | a | b | c | d |
|---|---|---|---|---|
| **18.** | 854 → <br> −165 → | 254 → <br> +529 → | 745 → <br> −286 → | 244 → <br> +398 → |

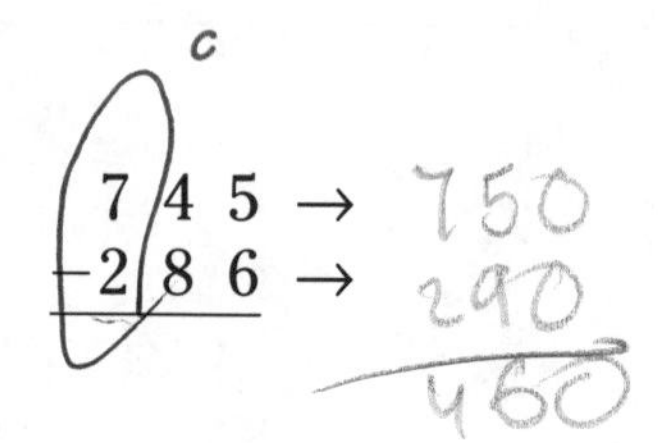

**Make a line graph to display the data in each table.**

**19.** **Baltimore Orioles Games Won**

| Year | 1995 | 1996 | 1997 | 1998 | 1999 |
|---|---|---|---|---|---|
| Wins | 71 | 88 | 98 | 79 | 78 |

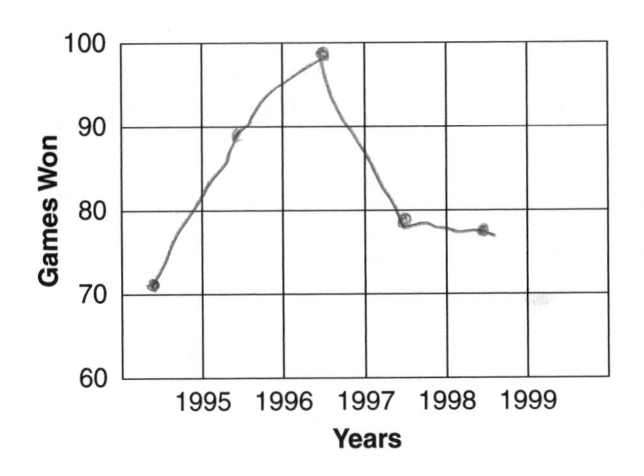


**20.** **Average Temperature Omaha, Nebraska**

| Month | Apr. | May | June | July | Aug. |
|---|---|---|---|---|---|
| Temp. | 52° | 62° | 72° | 77° | 74° |

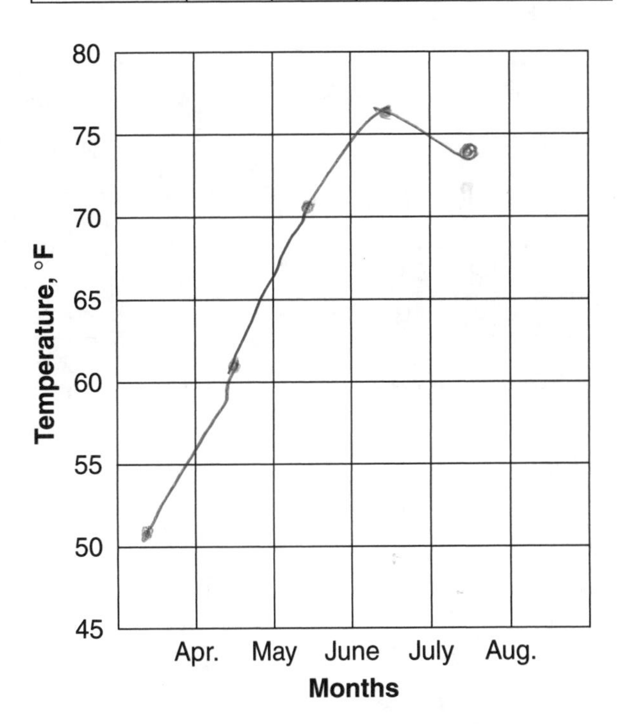


**Work backwards to solve each problem.**

**21.** Kelly has 47 model cars. Jamal has 58 model cars. Yesterday, Jamal traded 8 model cars to Kelly for 14 of her cars. How many cars did Kelly have before the trade?

Answer 73 cars ✓

**22.** Anita had $15 left after going shopping for the party. She bought food and drinks for $58. Then she spent $27 for decorations. How much money did Anita take shopping?

58
27
15
100

Answer $100

## Multiplication of One-digit Numbers

To multiply by one-digit numbers, use your basic multiplication facts.

**Find: 6 × 325**

Multiply 5 by 6 ones.

Regroup.

| | Th | H | T | O |
|---|---|---|---|---|
| | | | 3 | |
| | | 3 | 2 | 5 |
| × | | | | 6 |
| | | | | 0 |

Multiply 2 tens by 6 ones.

Regroup.

| | Th | H | T | O |
|---|---|---|---|---|
| | | 1 | 3 | |
| | | 3 | 2 | 5 |
| × | | | | 6 |
| | | | 5 | 0 |

Multiply 3 hundreds by 6 ones.

| | Th | H | T | O |
|---|---|---|---|---|
| | | 1 | 3 | |
| | | 3 | 2 | 5 |
| × | | | | 6 |
| | 1, | 9 | 5 | 0 |

**Multiply.**

| | a | b | c | d | e |
|---|---|---|---|---|---|
| 1. | 32 × 7 = 224 | 45 × 3 | 87 × 2 | 56 × 8 | 42 × 7 |
| 2. | 86 × 8 | 66 × 9 | 37 × 6 | 56 × 4 | 168 × 4 |
| 3. | 739 × 3 | 265 × 7 | 431 × 9 | 573 × 5 | |

# Multiplying Two-digit Numbers by Two-digit Numbers

To multiply two-digit numbers by two-digit numbers, line up the digits. Multiply the ones, then the tens. Write zeros as place holders. Add the partial products.

**Find: 36 × 46**

Multiply by 6 ones. Regroup.

| | Th | H | T | O |
|---|---|---|---|---|
| | | | 3 | |
| | | | 4 | 6 |
| × | | | 3 | 6 |
| | | 2 | 7 | 6 |

Write a zero place holder. Multiply by 3 tens. Regroup.

| | Th | H | T | O |
|---|---|---|---|---|
| | | | 1 | |
| | | | 4 | 6 |
| × | | | 3 | 6 |
| | | 2 | 7 | 6 |
| | 1, | 3 | 8 | 0 (zero place holder) |

Add the partial products.

| | Th | H | T | O |
|---|---|---|---|---|
| | | | 4 | 6 |
| × | | | 3 | 6 |
| | | 2 | 7 | 6 |
| + | 1, | 3 | 8 | 0 |
| | 1, | 6 | 5 | 6 |

**Multiply.**

**1.**

a.

| | Th | H | T | O |
|---|---|---|---|---|
| | | | 1 | |
| | | | 1 | 4 |
| × | | | 1 | 3 |
| | | | 4 | 2 |
| + | | 1 | 4 | 0 |
| | | 1 | 8 | 2 |

b. 41 × 22

c. 27 × 54

d. 32 × 67

**2.**

a. 28 × 15

b. 58 × 21

c. 65 × 42

d. 84 × 73

**3.**

a. 39 × 26

b. 51 × 19

c. 63 × 81

d. 92 × 55

# Multiplying Three-digit Numbers by Two-digit Numbers

Multiply three-digit numbers the same way you multiply two-digit numbers.

**Find: 69 × 618**

Multiply by 9 ones. Regroup.

| | TTh | Th | H | T | O |
|---|---|---|---|---|---|
| | | | 1 | 7 | |
| | | | 6 | 1 | 8 |
| × | | | | 6 | 9 |
| | | 5, | 5 | 6 | 2 |

Write a zero place holder. Multiply by 6 tens. Regroup.

| | TTh | Th | H | T | O |
|---|---|---|---|---|---|
| | | | 1 | 4 | |
| | | | 6 | 1 | 8 |
| × | | | | 6 | 9 |
| | | 5, | 5 | 6 | 2 |
| | 3 | 7, | 0 | 8 | 0 |

Add the partial products.

| | TTh | Th | H | T | O |
|---|---|---|---|---|---|
| | | | 6 | 1 | 8 |
| × | | | | 6 | 9 |
| | | 5, | 5 | 6 | 2 |
| + | 3 | 7, | 0 | 8 | 0 |
| | 4 | 2, | 6 | 4 | 2 |

**Multiply.**

| | a | b | c | d |
|---|---|---|---|---|
| **1.** | 741 × 25 = 3,705 + 14,820 = 18,525 | 912 × 19 | 158 × 29 | 226 × 16 |
| **2.** | 345 × 32 | 128 × 42 | 512 × 34 | 414 × 48 |

**Line up the digits. Then find the products.**

| | a | b |
|---|---|---|
| **3.** | 362 × 76 = ______ | 847 × 54 = ______ |

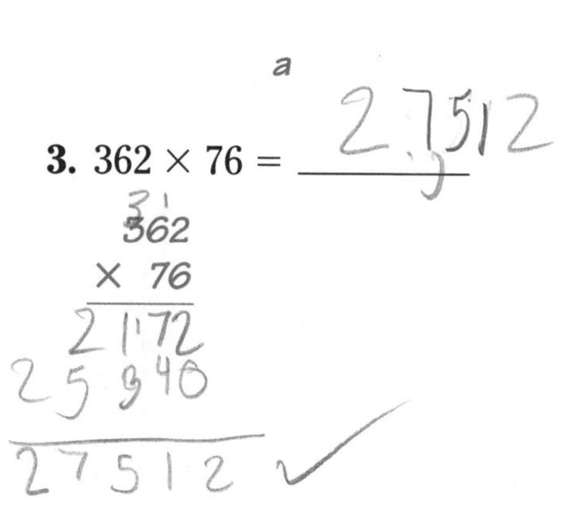

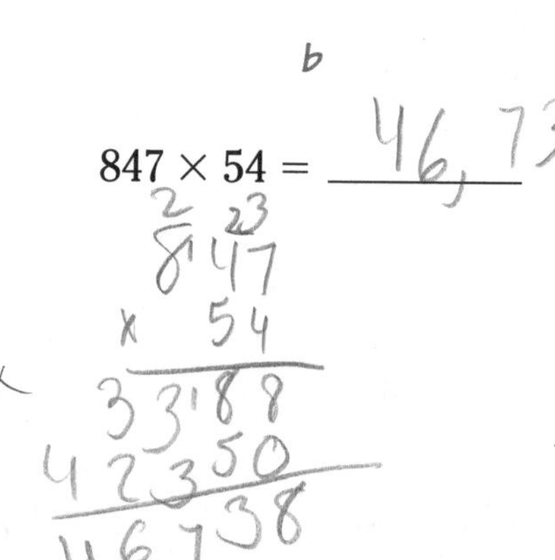

# Zeros in Multiplication

**Remember,**

- **the product of 0 and any number is 0.**
- **the sum of 0 and any number is that number.**

**Find: 27 × 608**

Multiply by 7 ones. Regroup.

| | TTh | Th | H | T | O |
|---|---|---|---|---|---|
| | | | | 5 | |
| | | | 6 | 0 | 8 |
| × | | | | 2 | 7 |
| | | 4, | 2 | 5 | 6 |

Write a zero place holder. Multiply by 2 tens. Regroup.

| | TTh | Th | H | T | O |
|---|---|---|---|---|---|
| | | | | 1 | |
| | | | 6 | 0 | 8 |
| × | | | | 2 | 7 |
| | | 4, | 2 | 5 | 6 |
| | 1 | 2, | 1 | 6 | 0 |

Add the partial products.

| | TTh | Th | H | T | O |
|---|---|---|---|---|---|
| | | | 6 | 0 | 8 |
| × | | | | 2 | 7 |
| | | 4, | 2 | 5 | 6 |
| + | 1 | 2, | 1 | 6 | 0 |
| | 1 | 6, | 4 | 1 | 6 |

**Multiply.**

| | a | b | c | d | e |
|---|---|---|---|---|---|
| 1. | 30 × 3 = 90 | 20 × 6 = 120 | 10 × 7 = 70 | 60 × 4 = 240 | 40 × 6 = 240 |
| 2. | 709 × 82 = 58,138 | 304 × 49 = 14,896 | 55 × 70 = 3850 | 48 × 20 = 960 | 14 × 30 = 420 |
| 3. | 507 × 20 = 10140 | 806 × 40 = 32240 | 390 × 60 = 23400 | 204 × 90 = 18360 | 100 × 20 = 2000 |

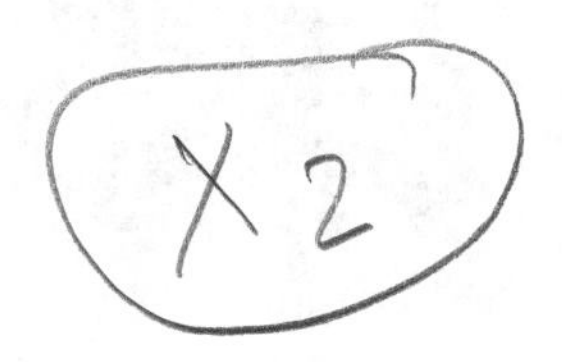

## Problem-Solving Method: Solve Multi-Step Problems

Many people think that one "dog year" is equal to seven "human years." But according to veterinarians, the first two years of a dog's life are equal to 35 human years. Every year after that is equal to three human years. Max is a dog. He is eight years old. How old is Max in human years?

**Understand the problem.**

- **What do you want to know?**
  Max's age in human years

- **What information is given?**
  First 2 dog years = 35 human years
  Every year after that = 3 human years
  Max is 8 years old.

**Plan how to solve it.**

- **What method can you use?**
  You can separate the problem into steps.

**Solve it.**

- **How can you use this method to solve the problem?**
  Subtract the first 2 years from his age. Multiply the remaining years by 3. Then add 35 years.

| Step 1 Subtract | Step 2 Multiply | Step 3 Add |
|---|---|---|
| 8 ← Max's age | 6 ← dog years | 35 ← first 2 years |
| −2 ← first 2 years | ×3 ← human years | +18 ← remaining 6 years |
| 6 years | 18 years | 53 years |

- **What is the answer?**
  Max is 53 years old in human years.

**Look back and check your answer.**

- **Is your answer reasonable?**
  You can add to check your multiplication.

  $35 + 3 + 3 + 3 + 3 + 3 + 3 = 53$

  The answer matches the sum.
  The answer is reasonable.

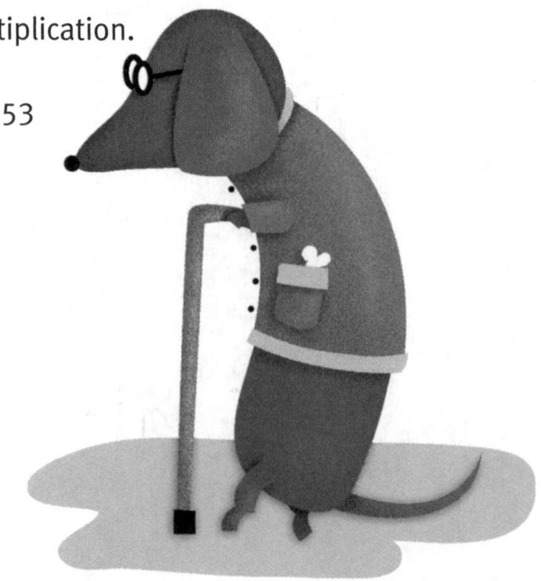

**Separate each problem into steps to solve.**

1. One egg has 75 calories. One slice of bacon has 38 calories. How many calories are in a breakfast of 2 eggs and 4 slices of bacon?

   Answer 302 calories

2. A bushel of apples weighs about 42 pounds. Bill's truck can carry 7,000 pounds. If he loads 150 bushels of apples, how many more pounds can the truck carry?

   Answer 700 more pounds

3. The football team needs $600 for new equipment. They washed 38 cars on Saturday for $15 each car. How much more money do they need?

   Answer $30

4. In an ordinary year, there are 365 days. In a leap year, there are 366 days. There are 24 hours in a day. How many more hours are there in one leap year than in one ordinary year?

   Answer 24 hours

5. A dolphin can swim 30 miles per hour. A sea lion can swim 25 miles per hour. If both animals swim for 5 hours, how much farther will the dolphin go?

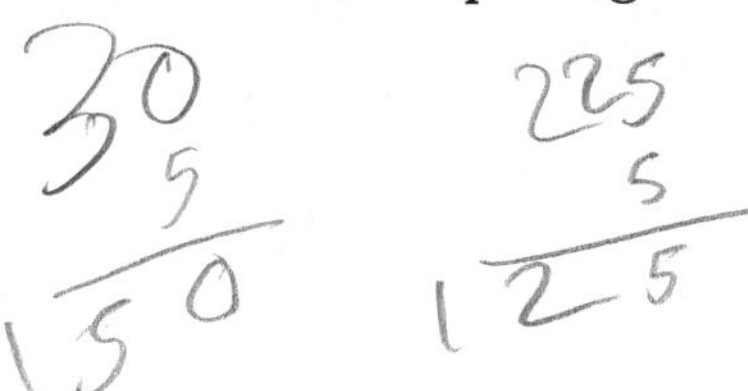

   Answer 25 miles

# Estimation of Products

To estimate products, round each **factor**. Then multiply the rounded factors.

**Find: 28 × 44**

Round each factor to the greatest place value. Multiply.

```
  4 4 →     4 0
× 2 8 →   × 3 0   ← 2 zeros
         1,2 0 0  ← 2 zeros
```

**Estimate the products.**

| | a | b | c | d |
|---|---|---|---|---|
| 1. | 32 → 30<br>×57 → ×60<br>1,800 | 18 → 20<br>×29 → 30<br>600 | 46 → 50<br>×13 → 10<br>500 | 65 → 70<br>×21 → 20<br>1400 |
| 2. | 73 → 70<br>×28 → 30<br>2100 | 84 → 80<br>×66 → 70<br>5600 | 57 → 60<br>×39 → 40<br>2400 | 43 → 40<br>×22 → 20<br>800 |
| 3. | 94 → 90<br>×35 → 40<br>3600 | 79 → 80<br>×18 → 20<br>1600 | 52 → 50<br>×39 → 40<br>2000 | 81 → 80<br>×24 → 20<br>1600 |

**Line up the digits. Then estimate the products.**

| | a | b | c |
|---|---|---|---|
| 4. | 27 × 55 1800<br>27 → 30<br>×55 → ×60<br>1800 | 86 × 12 900<br>90<br>10<br>900 | 48 × 33 1500<br>50<br>30<br>1500 |

# Multiplying Three-digit Numbers by Three-digit Numbers

To multiply three-digit numbers by three-digit numbers, line up the digits.
Multiply, starting with the ones digits. Write zeros as place holders.
Add the three partial products.

**Find: 342 × 576**

Multiply by 2 ones. Regroup.

| | Th | H | T | O |
|---|---|---|---|---|
| | | 1 | 1 | |
| | | 5 | 7 | 6 |
| × | | 3 | 4 | 2 |
| | 1, | 1 | 5 | 2 |

Write one zero. Multiply by 4 tens. Regroup.

| | TTh | Th | H | T | O |
|---|---|---|---|---|---|
| | | | 3 | 2 | |
| | | | 5 | 7 | 6 |
| × | | | 3 | 4 | 2 |
| | | 1, | 1 | 5 | 2 |
| | 2 | 3, | 0 | 4 | 0 |

Write two zeros. Multiply by 3 hundreds. Regroup.

| | HTh | TTh | Th | H | T | O |
|---|---|---|---|---|---|---|
| | | | | 2 | 1 | |
| | | | | 5 | 7 | 6 |
| × | | | | 3 | 4 | 2 |
| | | | 1, | 1 | 5 | 2 |
| | | 2 | 3, | 0 | 4 | 0 |
| | 1 | 7 | 2, | 8 | 0 | 0 |

Add.

| | HTh | TTh | Th | H | T | O |
|---|---|---|---|---|---|---|
| | | | | 5 | 7 | 6 |
| × | | | | 3 | 4 | 2 |
| | | | 1, | 1 | 5 | 2 |
| | | 2 | 3, | 0 | 4 | 0 |
| + | 1 | 7 | 2, | 8 | 0 | 0 |
| | 1 | 9 | 6, | 9 | 9 | 2 |

**Multiply.**

**1.**

a

| | TTh | Th | H | T | O |
|---|---|---|---|---|---|
| | | | 4 | 2 | 4 |
| × | | | 1 | 2 | 2 |
| | | | 8 | 4 | 8 |
| | | 8, | 4 | 8 | 0 |
| + | 4 | 2, | 4 | 0 | 0 |
| | 5 | 1, | 7 | 2 | 8 |

b

| | HTh | TTh | Th | H | T | O |
|---|---|---|---|---|---|---|
| | | | | 2 | 5 | 0 |
| × | | | | 4 | 3 | 6 |

c

| | HTh | TTh | Th | H | T | O |
|---|---|---|---|---|---|---|
| | | | | 5 | 0 | 9 |
| × | | | | 2 | 6 | 7 |

d

| | HTh | TTh | Th | H | T | O |
|---|---|---|---|---|---|---|
| | | | | 7 | 4 | 6 |
| × | | | | 8 | 9 | 1 |

**2.**

a

| | TTh | Th | H | T | O |
|---|---|---|---|---|---|
| | | | 2 | 3 | 2 |
| × | | | 2 | 3 | 2 |

b

| | HTh | TTh | Th | H | T | O |
|---|---|---|---|---|---|---|
| | | | | 5 | 4 | 0 |
| × | | | | 4 | 3 | 2 |

c

| | HTh | TTh | Th | H | T | O |
|---|---|---|---|---|---|---|
| | | | | 7 | 1 | 4 |
| × | | | | 3 | 6 | 9 |

d

| | HTh | TTh | Th | H | T | O |
|---|---|---|---|---|---|---|
| | | | | 9 | 1 | 3 |
| × | | | | 5 | 4 | 0 |

## Multiplication of Large Numbers

**To multiply large numbers, use the same steps you use to multiply smaller numbers.**

**Study these examples.**

Multiply by 6 ones.

| | HTh | TTh | Th | H | T | O |
|---|---|---|---|---|---|---|
| | | 2 | 3 | 1 | 1 | |
| | | 2 | 4, | 6 | 3 | 2 |
| × | | | | | | 6 |
| | 1 | 4 | 7, | 7 | 9 | 2 |

Multiply by 6 ones, 2 tens. Then add.

| | HTh | TTh | Th | H | T | O |
|---|---|---|---|---|---|---|
| | | | 4, | 6 | 7 | 1 |
| × | | | | | 2 | 6 |
| | | 2 | 8, | 0 | 2 | 6 |
| + | | 9 | 3, | 4 | 2 | 0 |
| | 1 | 2 | 1, | 4 | 4 | 6 |

Multiply by 2 ones, 3 tens. Then add.

| | M | HTh | TTh | Th | H | T | O |
|---|---|---|---|---|---|---|---|
| | | | 5 | 0, | 0 | 0 | 0 |
| × | | | | | | 3 | 2 |
| | | 1 | 0 | 0, | 0 | 0 | 0 |
| + | 1, | 5 | 0 | 0, | 0 | 0 | 0 |
| | 1, | 6 | 0 | 0, | 0 | 0 | 0 |

**Multiply.**

| | a | b | c | d |
|---|---|---|---|---|
| **1.** | 7,896 × 6 = 47,376 | 4,687 × 4 = 18748 | 2,468 × 7 = 17276 | 5,000 × 8 = 40000 |
| **2.** | 2,392 × 54: 9568 + 119600 = 129168 | 3,000 × 90 = 270000 | 53,404 × 16: 320424 + 534040 = 854464 | 42,000 × 19: 378000 + 420000 = 798000 |

**Line up the digits. Then find the products.**

| | a | b | c |
|---|---|---|---|
| **3.** | 2 × 4,653 = 9306 | 9 × 38,641 = 347769 | 14 × 5,207 = [illegible] |

4,653
× 2
9306

38641
× 9
347769

5207
× 14
20828
52070
72898

## Problem-Solving Method: Identify Extra Information

Niagara Falls is on the border between the United States and Canada, with about 85 percent of the water on the Canadian side. Every second, 2,830 cubic meters of water pour over Niagara Falls. The energy from the water is used to power 13 generators in New York. How much water goes over the falls every minute?

**Understand the problem.**

- **What do you want to know?**
  how much water goes over Niagara Falls every minute (60 seconds)

**Plan how to solve it.**

- **What method can you use?**
  You can identify extra information that is not needed to solve the problem.

**Solve it.**

- **How can you use this method to solve the problem?**
  Reread the problem. Cross out any unnecessary words. Then you can focus on the facts needed to solve the problem.

> ~~Niagara Falls is on the border between the United States and Canada, with about 85 percent of the water on the Canadian side~~. Every second, 2,830 cubic meters of water pour over Niagara Falls. ~~The energy from the water is used to power 13 generators in New York~~. How much water goes over the falls every minute?

- **What is the answer?**

  2,830 × 60 = 169,800

  Every minute, 169,800 cubic meters of water pour over Niagara Falls.

**Look back and check your answer.**

- **Is your answer reasonable?**
  You can estimate to check your answer.

$$\begin{array}{r} 2{,}830 \\ \times \quad 60 \\ \hline \end{array} \longrightarrow \begin{array}{r} 3{,}000 \\ \times \quad 60 \\ \hline 180{,}000 \end{array}$$

The estimate is close to the answer. The answer is reasonable.

**In each problem, cross out the extra information. Then solve the problem.**

1. Cheetahs are found in Africa and Asia. They are the fastest animals in the world, reaching up to 70 miles per hour. Cheetahs are usually less than 3 feet tall and weigh about 110 pounds. How far can a cheetah run in 5 hours?

Answer 350 miles

2. Each square inch of human skin has 19 million cells, 60 hairs, 90 oil glands, 19 feet of blood vessels, and 625 sweat glands. If the palm of your hand covers 16 square inches, how many sweat glands are in your palm?

Answer 10,000 sweat glands

3. One honeybee would have to visit over 2,000,000 flowers and travel 55,000 miles to collect enough nectar to produce 1 pound of honey. How many miles would a honeybee have to fly for 3 pounds of honey?

Answer 165,000 miles

4. One million dollars in $1 bills would weigh about one ton, or 2,000 pounds. Placed in a pile, it would be 360 feet high—as tall as 60 average adults standing on top of each other. How many pounds would $5,000,000 in $1 bills weigh?

Answer 10,000 lbs

5. A mile on the ocean and a mile on land are not the same distance. On the ocean, a nautical mile measures 6,080 feet. A land mile is 5,280 feet. If a cruise ship sails 75 nautical miles, how many feet does it travel?

Answer 456000 ft.

# Problem Solving

**Solve.**

1. People dream an average of 5 times a night. How many times do you dream in 1 year? (365 days)

   Answer ______________________

2. Greenland is the largest island in the world—about 21 times the size of Iceland. Iceland covers 39,800 square miles. About how many square miles does Greenland cover?

   Answer ______________________

3. Craig drove 12 hours at an average speed of 55 miles per hour. Estimate how many miles he traveled.

   Answer ______________________

4. From 1997 to 2000, people making minimum wage and working 40 hours a week earned $10,712 a year. How much did they earn in the 3 years altogether?

   Answer ______________________

5. The theater seats 375 people. There will be 428 shows this year. How many people can see a show this year?

   Answer ______________________

6. Noah Webster spent 36 years writing his dictionary. There are 12 months in a year. How many months did Webster spend writing the dictionary?

   Answer ______________________

7. The Concord jet flies 2,222 kilometers per hour. How far can the Concord travel in 8 hours?

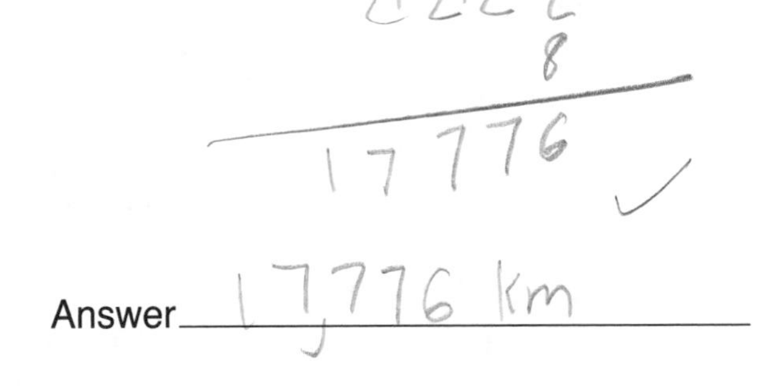

   Answer ______________________

**Multiply.**

| | a | b | c | d |
|---|---|---|---|---|
| 1. | $60 \times 7$ | $90 \times 4$ | $700 \times 200$ | $830 \times 463$ |
| 2. | $2,605 \times 4$ | $4,891 \times 36$ | $2,005 \times 87$ | $11,847 \times 42$ |

**Line up the digits. Then find the products.**

| | a | b | c |
|---|---|---|---|
| 3. | $427 \times 906 =$ ______ | $313 \times 211 =$ ______ | $128 \times 975 =$ ______ |
| 4. | $3 \times 46,168 =$ ______ | $4 \times 21,741 =$ ______ | $20 \times 2,403 =$ ______ |

**Estimate the products.**

| | a | b | c | d |
|---|---|---|---|---|
| 5. | $62 \rightarrow$ <br> $\times 17 \rightarrow$ | $93 \rightarrow$ <br> $\times 42 \rightarrow$ | $38 \rightarrow$ <br> $\times 26 \rightarrow$ | $35 \rightarrow$ <br> $\times 46 \rightarrow$ |
| 6. | $25 \rightarrow$ <br> $\times 38 \rightarrow$ | $87 \rightarrow$ <br> $\times 14 \rightarrow$ | $64 \rightarrow$ <br> $\times 71 \rightarrow$ | $47 \rightarrow$ <br> $\times 82 \rightarrow$ |

# UNIT 2 Review

**Separate each problem into steps to solve.**

**7.** A whippet can run 36 miles per hour. A greyhound can run 40 miles per hour. If both dogs run for 3 hours, how much farther will the greyhound go?

40 × 3 = 120   36 × 3 = 108

Answer 12 miles

**8.** Every day there are 36 flights to Paris and 22 flights to New York from Heathrow Airport in London. Each plane holds about 130 passengers. How many people can fly to Paris or New York from Heathrow each day?

Answer Paris: 4680 NY: 2860

**9.** The Empire State Building in New York is hit by lightning about 100 times a year. The building opened in 1931. About how many times was it hit by lightning by the year 2000? (69 years)

Answer 6,900 times

**In each problem, cross out the extra information. Then solve the problem.**

**10.** ~~The gray kangaroo is the largest kangaroo in the world~~. It stands 7 feet tall and weighs 200 pounds. Gray kangaroos can reach speeds of 43 miles per hour and cover 29 feet with each hop. How many feet can a gray kangaroo cover in 25 hops?

Answer 725 ft.

**11.** During World War II, the United States Navy built the world's first floating ice cream parlor. While cruising the Pacific Ocean, this ship was capable of making 85 gallons of ice cream every minute. How many gallons of ice cream could they make every hour? (1 hour = 60 minutes)

Answer 5100 gallons

## One-digit Divisors

To divide by a one-digit divisor, first decide on a **trial quotient**. Then multiply and subtract.

**Remember, if your trial quotient is too large or too small, try another number.**

**Find: 378 ÷ 6**

| Divide. | Multiply and subtract. | Multiply and subtract. | Check: |
|---|---|---|---|
| H T O<br>6 ) 3 7 8<br>3 < 6<br>6 does not go into 3.<br>Move to the next place value. | H T O<br>6<br>6 ) 3 7 8<br>−3 6<br>1 8<br>6)37 is about 6. | H T O<br>quotient → 6 3<br>divisor → 6 ) 3 7 8<br>−3 6<br>1 8<br>−1 8<br>0<br>6)18 = 3 | Multiply the quotient by the divisor.<br>63<br>× 6<br>378 |

**Divide.**

| | a | b | c | d | e |
|---|---|---|---|---|---|
| 1. | T O<br>1 2<br>8 ) 9 6<br>−8 ↓<br>1 6<br>−1 6<br>0 | T O<br>4 ) 7 6 | T O<br>3 ) 8 1 | H T O<br>2 ) 9 4 6 | H T O<br>8 ) 9 6 8 |
| 2. | H T O<br>2 ) 1 9 6 | H T O<br>6 ) 3 3 6 | H T O<br>7 ) 1 5 4 | H T O<br>9 ) 8 3 7 | H T O<br>3 ) 4 2 3 |

## One-digit Divisors with Remainders

To divide, first decide on a trial quotient. Multiply and subtract. Then write the **remainder** in the quotient.

**Find:** 749 ÷ 5

Multiply and subtract.

```
H|T|O
 1
5)7 4 9
 -5
  2 4
```

5)7 is about 1.

Multiply and subtract.

```
H|T|O
 1 4
5)7 4 9
 -5
  2 4
 -2 0
    4 9
```

5)24 is about 4.

Multiply and subtract. Write the remainder in the quotient.

```
H|T|O
 1 4 9 R4
5)7 4 9
 -5
  2 4
 -2 0
    4 9
  - 4 5
      4
```

5)49 is about 9.

Check:

Multiply the quotient by the divisor.

Add the remainder.

```
  149
×   5
  745
+   4
  749
```

**Divide.**

| | a | b | c | d |
|---|---|---|---|---|
| **1.** | 6)67 = 11 R1 (−6, 7, −6, 1) | 3)44 | 5)76 | 7)88 |
| **2.** | 8)10 | 4)139 | 8)6,911 | 7)1,013 |

# Zeros in Quotients

To divide, decide on a trial quotient. Then multiply and subtract. Remember to divide every time you bring down a number. When you cannot divide, write a zero in the quotient as a **place holder**.

**Find: 325 ÷ 3**

Multiply and subtract.

| H | T | O |
|---|---|---|
| 1 | | |
| 3)3 | 2 | 5 |
| −3 | ↓ | |
| 0 | 2 | |

$3\overline{)3}$ = 1

Multiply and subtract.

| H | T | O |
|---|---|---|
| 1 | 0 | |
| 3)3 | 2 | 5 |
| −3 | | |
| | 2 | |
| | −0 | ↓ |
| | 2 | 5 |

← Write a zero in the quotient as a place holder.

$3\overline{)2}$ = 0

Multiply and subtract.

| H | T | O |
|---|---|---|
| 1 | 0 | 8 R1 |
| 3)3 | 2 | 5 |
| −3 | | |
| | 2 | |
| | −0 | |
| | 2 | 5 |
| | −2 | 4 |
| | | 1 |

$3\overline{)25}$ is about 8.

**Divide.**

| | a | b | c | d |
|---|---|---|---|---|
| 1. | 109 R4<br>5)549<br>−5<br>4<br>−0<br>49<br>−45<br>4 | 2)815 | 7)738 | 3)923 |
| 2. | 3)150 | 5)202 | 9)7,234 | 8)4,832 |

# Two-digit Divisors: Multiples of 10

To divide by multiples of ten, choose a trial quotient.
Then multiply and subtract.

**Find: 760 ÷ 60**

| Multiply and subtract. | Multiply and subtract. | Check: |
|---|---|---|
| $\begin{array}{r} 1\phantom{60} \\ 60\overline{)760} \\ -60\phantom{0} \\ \hline 160 \end{array}$ | $\begin{array}{r} 12\text{ R}40 \\ 60\overline{)760} \\ -60\phantom{0} \\ \hline 160 \\ -120 \\ \hline 40 \end{array}$ | $\begin{array}{r} 12 \\ \times 60 \\ \hline 720 \\ +40 \\ \hline 760 \end{array}$ |
| **Think:** $6\overline{)7}$ is about 1. So, $60\overline{)76}$ is about 1. Put the 1 above the 6. | **Think:** $6\overline{)16}$ is about 2. So, $60\overline{)160}$ is about 2. | |

**Divide.**

| | a | b | c | d |
|---|---|---|---|---|
| **1.** | $\begin{array}{r} 18\text{ R}37 \\ 50\overline{)937} \\ -50\phantom{7} \\ \hline 437 \\ -400 \\ \hline 37 \end{array}$ | $30\overline{)978}$ | $20\overline{)860}$ | $40\overline{)885}$ |
| **2.** | $80\overline{)1,040}$ | $70\overline{)2,620}$ | $60\overline{)1,560}$ | $90\overline{)4,430}$ |

**Set up the problems. Then find the quotients.**

| | a | b | c |
|---|---|---|---|
| **3.** | 1,285 ÷ 20 = ________ | 1,670 ÷ 60 = ________ | 3,760 ÷ 80 = ________ |
| | $20\overline{)1,285}$ | | |

## Problem-Solving Method: Choose an Operation

Every week, 847 tons of dust from outer space enter Earth's atmosphere. If the dust could be shoveled into one pile, it would be as big as a 14-story building. How many tons of dust from outer space enter the atmosphere every day?

**Understand the problem.**

- **What do you want to know?**
  how much dust enters the atmosphere every day

- **What information do you know?**
  847 tons enter every week.
  There are 7 days in a week.

**Plan how to solve it.**

- **What method can you use?**
  You can choose the operation needed to solve the problem.

| Unequal Groups | Equal Groups |
|---|---|
| **Add** to combine unequal groups. | **Multiply** to combine equal groups. |
| **Subtract** to separate into unequal groups. | **Divide** to separate into equal groups. |

**Solve it.**

- **How can you use this method to solve the problem?**
  Since you need to separate the total, 847 tons, into 7 equal groups, you can divide to find how many tons will be in each group.

$$\begin{array}{r} 121 \\ 7\overline{)847} \\ -7\phantom{00} \\ \hline 14\phantom{0} \\ -14\phantom{0} \\ \hline 07 \\ -\ 7 \\ \hline 0 \end{array}$$

- **What is the answer?**
  Every day, 121 tons of dust enter Earth's atmosphere.

**Look back and check your answer.**

- **Is your answer reasonable?**
  You can check division with multiplication.

$$\begin{array}{r} 121 \\ \times\quad 7 \\ \hline 847 \end{array}$$

The product matches the dividend.
The answer is reasonable.

**Choose an operation to solve each problem. Then solve the problem.**

1. Tuna swim at a steady speed of 9 miles per hour. They never stop during their entire lives. How many hours does it take a tuna to swim 216 miles?

Operation ______________________

Answer ______________________

2. Zippers were invented in 1891. Velcro was invented in 1948. How many years passed between the two inventions?

Operation ______________________

Answer ______________________

3. An ant can lift 50 times its own weight. Ted weighs 165 pounds. If Ted were as strong as an ant, how much could he lift?

Operation ______________________

Answer ______________________

4. The average two-year-old learns 112 new words a week. How many words does a two-year-old learn each day? (1 week = 7 days)

Operation ______________________

Answer ______________________

5. Pluto is the slowest planet. It travels around the sun at a speed of 10,600 miles per hour. How far does Pluto travel in 8 hours?

Operation ______________________

Answer ______________________

# Estimating Quotients

To estimate quotients, use rounded numbers.

**Estimate:** $345 \div 5$

Round the dividend until you can use a basic fact. Divide.

$5\overline{)345}$ $345 \div 5$

**Think:** $35 \div 5 = 7$ $350 \div 5 = 70$

**Estimate:** $828 \div 23$

Round the dividend and the divisor until you can use a basic fact. Divide.

$23\overline{)828}$ $828 \div 23$

**Think:** $8 \div 2 = 4$ $800 \div 20 = 40$

**Round the dividends to estimate the quotients.**

| | a | b | c |
|---|---|---|---|
| 1. | $272 \div 3$ ↓ ↓ $270 \div 3 = 90$ | $419 \div 7$ ↓ ↓ | $363 \div 9$ ↓ ↓ |
| 2. | $5\overline{)418}$ → $5\overline{)400}$ = 80 | $3\overline{)167}$ → | $6\overline{)233}$ → |

**Round the dividends and the divisors to estimate the quotients.**

| | a | b | c |
|---|---|---|---|
| 3. | $756 \div 36$ ↓ ↓ $800 \div 40 = 20$ | $924 \div 28$ ↓ ↓ | $578 \div 17$ ↓ ↓ |
| 4. | $52\overline{)988}$ → | $31\overline{)899}$ → | $43\overline{)774}$ → |

# Trial Quotients

When you divide, you may have to try several quotients. Estimate to choose a **trial quotient**. Then multiply and subtract. If it is too large or too small, try again.

**Find: 928 ÷ 32**

| Estimate to choose a trial quotient. | Multiply and subtract. | Try a smaller number. Multiply and subtract. | Finish the problem. |
|---|---|---|---|
| $32\overline{)928}$ | $\begin{array}{r} 3 \\ 32\overline{)928} \\ -96 \end{array}$ | $\begin{array}{r} 2 \\ 32\overline{)928} \\ -64 \\ 28 \end{array}$ | $\begin{array}{r} 29 \\ 32\overline{)928} \\ -64 \\ 288 \\ -288 \\ 0 \end{array}$ |
| **Think:** 32 rounds to 30. $3\overline{)9}$ = 3. So, $32\overline{)92}$ is about 3. | Since 96 > 92, 3 is too large. | Since 28 < 32, 2 is correct. | |

**Write *too large*, *too small*, or *correct* for each trial quotient. Then write the correct trial quotient.**

| | *a* | | *b* | |
|---|---|---|---|---|
| **1.** | $\begin{array}{r} 4 \\ 22\overline{)858} \\ -88 \end{array}$ | *too large* ___ <br> *3* ___ | $\begin{array}{r} 2 \\ 26\overline{)795} \\ -52 \end{array}$ | ___ <br> ___ |
| **2.** | $\begin{array}{r} 3 \\ 31\overline{)907} \end{array}$ | ___ <br> ___ | $\begin{array}{r} 7 \\ 51\overline{)3{,}542} \end{array}$ | ___ <br> ___ |
| **3.** | $\begin{array}{r} 7 \\ 45\overline{)3{,}688} \end{array}$ | ___ <br> ___ | $\begin{array}{r} 5 \\ 87\overline{)4{,}241} \end{array}$ | ___ <br> ___ |

## Trial Quotients

**Write *too large, too small,* or *correct* for each trial quotient. Then write the correct trial quotient.**

| | a | | b | |
|---|---|---|---|---|
| 1. | $24\overline{)432}$ trial quotient 2 | ______ ______ | $29\overline{)232}$ trial quotient 7 | ______ ______ |
| 2. | $44\overline{)836}$ trial quotient 2 | ______ ______ | $67\overline{)469}$ trial quotient 6 | ______ ______ |
| 3. | $32\overline{)1{,}824}$ trial quotient 6 | ______ ______ | $13\overline{)4{,}056}$ trial quotient 4 | ______ ______ |
| 4. | $55\overline{)3{,}850}$ trial quotient 6 | ______ ______ | $25\overline{)2{,}175}$ trial quotient 7 | ______ ______ |
| 5. | $44\overline{)16{,}808}$ trial quotient 4 | ______ ______ | $85\overline{)51{,}935}$ trial quotient 5 | ______ ______ |

# Two-digit Divisors

To divide by a two-digit divisor, decide on a trial quotient. Multiply and subtract. Write the remainder in the quotient.

**Find: 569 ÷ 43**

Choose a trial quotient.

$$43\overline{)569}$$

**Think:** $4\overline{)5}$ is about 1. So, $43\overline{)56}$ is about 1.

Multiply and subtract.

$$\begin{array}{r} 1\phantom{9} \\ 43\overline{)569} \\ -43\phantom{9} \\ \hline 139 \end{array}$$

**Think:** $4\overline{)13}$ is about 3. So, $43\overline{)139}$ is about 3.

Multiply and subtract.

$$\begin{array}{r} 13 \text{ R}10 \\ 43\overline{)569} \\ -43\phantom{9} \\ \hline 139 \\ -129 \\ \hline 10 \end{array}$$

Check:

$$\begin{array}{r} 13 \\ \times 43 \\ \hline 559 \\ +10 \\ \hline 569 \end{array}$$

**Divide.**

| | a | b | c |
|---|---|---|---|
| 1. | $45\overline{)657}$ = 14 R27 ($-45$, 207, $-180$, 27) | $38\overline{)836}$ | $61\overline{)954}$ |
| 2. | $75\overline{)735}$ | $52\overline{)126}$ | $91\overline{)382}$ |
| 3. | $36\overline{)11{,}669}$ | $53\overline{)22{,}161}$ | $17\overline{)11{,}483}$ |

# Two-digit Divisors

**Divide.**

| | a | b | c | d |
|---|---|---|---|---|
| **1.** | $12\overline{)88}$ | $13\overline{)65}$ | $16\overline{)96}$ | $17\overline{)54}$ |
| **2.** | $15\overline{)465}$ | $32\overline{)672}$ | $41\overline{)839}$ | $24\overline{)944}$ |
| **3.** | $82\overline{)1{,}312}$ | $43\overline{)2{,}200}$ | $26\overline{)1{,}898}$ | $17\overline{)5{,}176}$ |
| **4.** | $55\overline{)17{,}270}$ | $38\overline{)19{,}927}$ | $74\overline{)30{,}313}$ | $63\overline{)10{,}584}$ |

**Set up the problems. Then find the quotients.**

| | a | b | c |
|---|---|---|---|
| **5.** | $38 \div 12 =$ ________ | $882 \div 42 =$ ________ | $931 \div 71 =$ ________ |
| | $12\overline{)38}$ | | |

## Problem-Solving Method: Write a Number Sentence

In 1999, *Orbiter 3* became the first balloon to travel around the entire world. The journey, which began in Switzerland, lasted 19 days and covered a distance of 26,600 miles. On average, how many miles a day did the balloon fly?

**Understand the problem.**

- **What do you want to know?**
  the average number of miles the balloon flew each day

- **What information is given?**
  The balloon flew a total of 26,600 miles in 19 days.

**Plan how to solve it.**

- **What method can you use?**
  You can write a number sentence to model the problem.

**Solve it.**

- **How can you use this method to solve the problem?**
  You want to separate the total miles into 19 even groups.
  So, write a division number sentence.

$$26{,}600 \div 19 = \underline{\qquad}$$

26,600 → total miles; 19 → number of days; blank → miles per day

$$\begin{array}{r} 1{,}400 \\ 19\overline{)26{,}600} \\ -19\phantom{,000} \\ \hline 7\,6\phantom{00} \\ -7\,6\phantom{00} \\ \hline 000 \end{array}$$

- **What is the answer?**
  The balloon flew an average of 1,400 miles each day.

**Look back and check your answer.**

- **Is your answer reasonable?**
  You can check division with multiplication.

$$\begin{array}{r} 1{,}400 \\ \times \quad 19 \\ \hline 12{,}600 \\ +14{,}000 \\ \hline 26{,}600 \end{array}$$

The product matches the dividend.
The answer is reasonable.

**Write a number sentence to solve each problem.**

1. Mexico City is one of the fastest growing cities in the world. If the population there increased by 15,183 people every week, how many more people would be in Mexico City every day? (1 week = 7 days)

   Answer ______________________

2. A sheepdog's sense of smell is 44 times better than a human's. If a person can smell a hamburger cooking from 12 feet away, how far away can the sheepdog be and still smell it?

   Answer ______________________

3. China has more school days than any other nation. Students there go to school 251 days a year. Japan is second, with 243 school days. How many more days a year do students in China go to school than students in Japan?

   Answer ______________________

4. The highest mountain on Earth, Mount Everest, is 29,035 feet tall. K2 is the world's second highest mountain. It is 28,250 feet tall. What is the difference between the two mountains?

   Answer ______________________

5. The average human heart rate is 70 beats per minute. How many times does a human heart beat per hour? (1 hour = 60 minutes)

   Answer ______________________

# UNIT 3 Review

**Divide.**

| | a | b | c | d |
|---|---|---|---|---|
| **1.** | $4\overline{)92}$ | $8\overline{)600}$ | $5\overline{)295}$ | $9\overline{)108}$ |
| **2.** | $3\overline{)50}$ | $6\overline{)561}$ | $7\overline{)425}$ | $2\overline{)1{,}014}$ |
| **3.** | $7\overline{)1{,}502}$ | $4\overline{)3{,}685}$ | $8\overline{)2{,}439}$ | $5\overline{)7{,}621}$ |
| **4.** | $20\overline{)840}$ | $30\overline{)1{,}050}$ | $70\overline{)6{,}350}$ | $80\overline{)1{,}608}$ |

**Set up the problems. Then find the quotients.**

| | a | b | c |
|---|---|---|---|
| **5.** | $84 \div 4 =$ ______ | $695 \div 5 =$ ______ | $368 \div 8 =$ ______ |
| **6.** | $46 \div 7 =$ ______ | $1{,}465 \div 30 =$ ______ | $2{,}690 \div 50 =$ ______ |

## UNIT 3 Review

**Round the dividends to estimate the quotients.**

| | a | b | c |
|---|---|---|---|
| 7. | $8\overline{)450}$ | $7\overline{)205}$ | $9\overline{)342}$ |

**Round the dividends and the divisors to estimate the quotients.**

| | a | b | c |
|---|---|---|---|
| 8. | $57\overline{)624}$ | $47\overline{)972}$ | $23\overline{)642}$ |

**Write *too large, too small,* or *correct* for each trial quotient. Then write the correct trial quotient.**

| | a | | b | |
|---|---|---|---|---|
| 9. | $\begin{array}{r} 7 \\ 72\overline{)5{,}109} \end{array}$ | ______________ ______________ | $\begin{array}{r} 8 \\ 42\overline{)3{,}287} \end{array}$ | ______________ ______________ |
| 10. | $\begin{array}{r} 7 \\ 31\overline{)2{,}527} \end{array}$ | ______________ ______________ | $\begin{array}{r} 4 \\ 51\overline{)1{,}624} \end{array}$ | ______________ ______________ |

**Divide.**

| | a | b | c | d |
|---|---|---|---|---|
| 11. | $38\overline{)988}$ | $64\overline{)1{,}344}$ | $42\overline{)1{,}600}$ | $57\overline{)3{,}673}$ |

**Set up the problems. Then find the quotients.**

| | a | b | c |
|---|---|---|---|
| 12. | $65 \div 13 =$ ______ | $649 \div 31 =$ ______ | $823 \div 47 =$ ______ |

**Choose an operation to solve each problem. Then solve the problem.**

**13.** It takes about 4 pounds of worms to eat a pound of garbage. How many pounds of worms are needed to eat 500 pounds of garbage?

Operation ____________________

Answer ____________________

**14.** An adult's small intestine is about 300 inches long. How long is that in feet? (1 foot = 12 inches)

Operation ____________________

Answer ____________________

**Write a number sentence to solve each problem.**

**15.** Every week, about 1,162 square miles of tropical rain forests are cut down. How many square miles are cut down every day?

Answer ____________________

**16.** One hour of bicycling burns about 210 calories. Steve rode his bike for 3 hours. About how many calories did he burn?

Answer ____________________

**17.** There are 167 steps from ground level to the top of the Statue of Liberty's pedestal. There are 168 steps from the pedestal to her head. How many steps are there from the ground to the Statue of Liberty's head?

Answer ____________________

## Meaning of Fractions

A **fraction** names part of a whole. This circle has 3 equal parts. Each part is $\frac{1}{3}$ of the circle. Two of the three equal parts are shaded green.

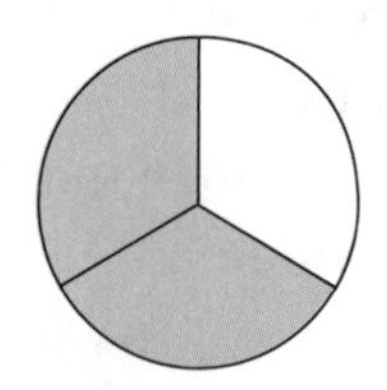

**We read $\frac{2}{3}$ as two-thirds.**

**numerator → 2 — two green parts**
**denominator → 3 — three parts in all**

A fraction also names part of a group. Three of the five flowers are red.

**3 — three red flowers**
**5 — five flowers in all**

**Three-fifths are red.**

**Write the fraction and the word name for the part that is shaded.**

| | a | b | c |
|---|---|---|---|
| **1.** | 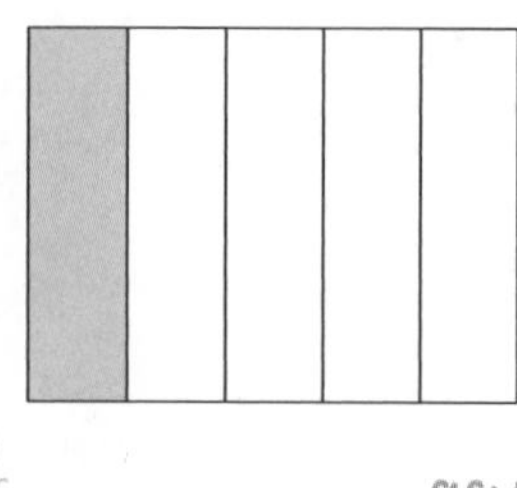 | 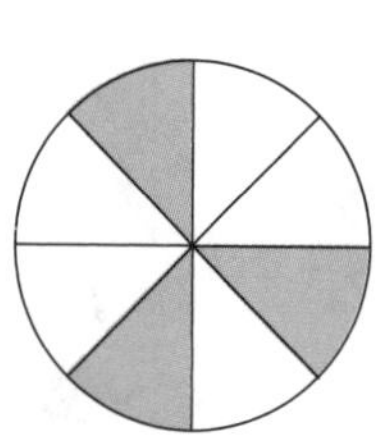 | 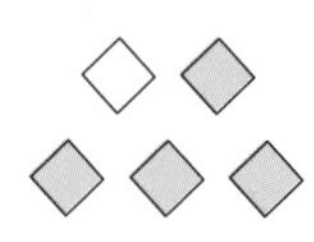 |
| | $\frac{1}{5}$ or one-fifth | ____ or ________ | ____ or ________ |

**Write the fraction for the word name.**

| | a | b | c |
|---|---|---|---|
| **2.** | two-sevenths $\frac{2}{7}$ | three-fourths ________ | six-ninths ________ |

**Write the word name for the fraction.**

| | a | b | c |
|---|---|---|---|
| **3.** | $\frac{5}{8}$ five-eighths | $\frac{4}{7}$ ________ | $\frac{1}{4}$ ________ |

**Write the fraction and the word name for the part that is shaded.**

| | a | b | c |
|---|---|---|---|
| **4.** | 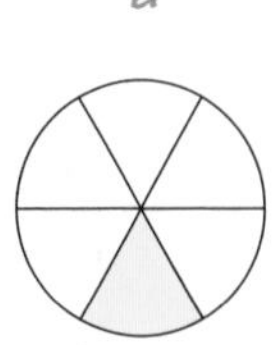 | 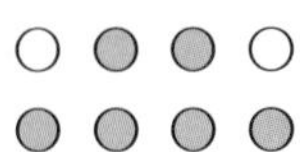 | 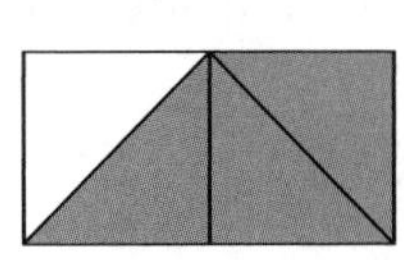 |
| | ______ or ______________ | ______ or ______________ | ______ or ______________ |

**Write the fraction for the word name.**

| | a | b | c |
|---|---|---|---|
| **5.** | nine-tenths ______________ | six-sixths ______________ | two-eighths ______________ |
| **6.** | five-sevenths ______________ | ten-twelfths ______________ | four-ninths ______________ |

**Write the word name for the fraction.**

| | a | b | c |
|---|---|---|---|
| **7.** | $\frac{1}{3}$ ______________ | $\frac{7}{9}$ ______________ | $\frac{5}{5}$ ______________ |
| **8.** | $\frac{6}{7}$ ______________ | $\frac{3}{10}$ ______________ | $\frac{9}{12}$ ______________ |

**There are 7 days in a week. Each day is $\frac{1}{7}$ week. Write the following as a fraction of a week. Write the word name for the fraction.**

| | a | b | c |
|---|---|---|---|
| **9.** | 4 days = $\frac{4}{7}$ week | 5 days = ________ week | 2 days = ________ week |
| | four-sevenths | ______________ | ______________ |

**There are 20 nickels in a dollar. Each nickel is $\frac{1}{20}$ dollar. Write the following as a fraction of a dollar. Write the word name for the fraction.**

| | a | b | c |
|---|---|---|---|
| **10.** | 6 nickels = $\frac{6}{20}$ dollar | 11 nickels = ________ dollar | 8 nickels = ________ dollar |
| | six-twentieths | ______________ | ______________ |

# Equivalent Fractions

**Equivalent fractions** have the same value. Compare the circles. The shaded part of one circle is equal to the shaded part of the other circle. What part of each circle is shaded?

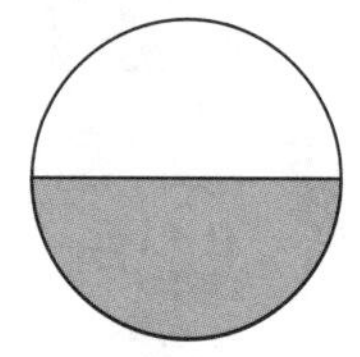

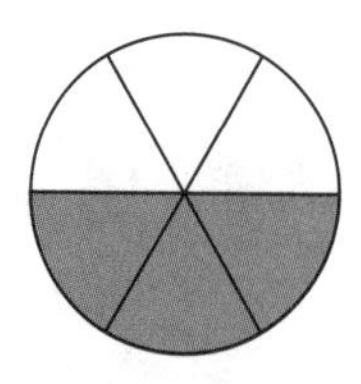

**$\frac{1}{2}$ of the circle is shaded.** **$\frac{3}{6}$ of the circle is shaded.**

**$\frac{1}{2}$ and $\frac{3}{6}$ are equivalent fractions. $\frac{1}{2} = \frac{3}{6}$**

**The pizza at the right is divided into 8 equal parts.**
**Each part is $\frac{1}{8}$ of the figure.**
**Write the equivalent fractions.**

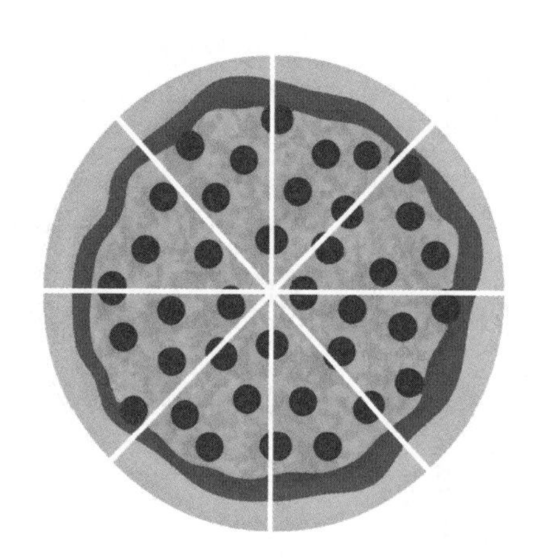

1. How many $\frac{1}{8}$ parts are in $\frac{1}{4}$ of the figure? 2 $\frac{1}{4} = \frac{2}{8}$

2. How many $\frac{1}{8}$ parts are in $\frac{1}{2}$ of the figure? ______ $\frac{1}{2} = \frac{\phantom{0}}{8}$

3. How many $\frac{1}{8}$ parts are in $\frac{3}{4}$ of the figure? ______ $\frac{3}{4} = \frac{\phantom{0}}{8}$

4. How many $\frac{1}{8}$ parts are in $\frac{2}{4}$ of the figure? ______ $\frac{2}{4} = \frac{\phantom{0}}{8}$

**Write two equivalent fractions for the shaded part of each figure.**

a b

5. 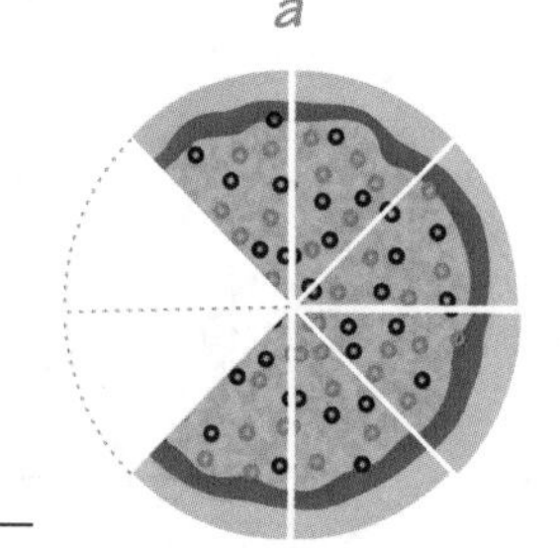

$\frac{3}{4} = \frac{6}{8}$

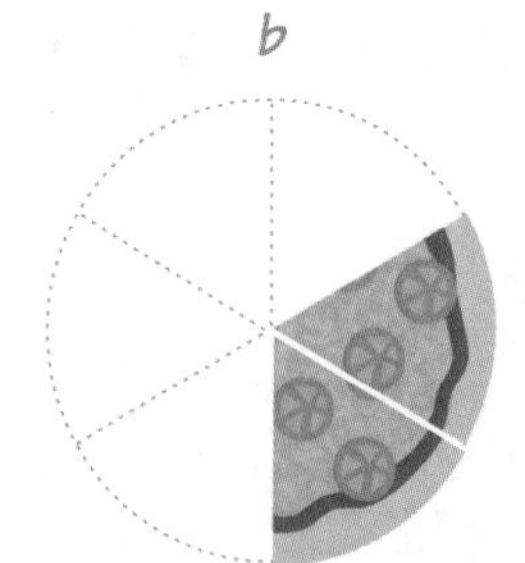

______

6. 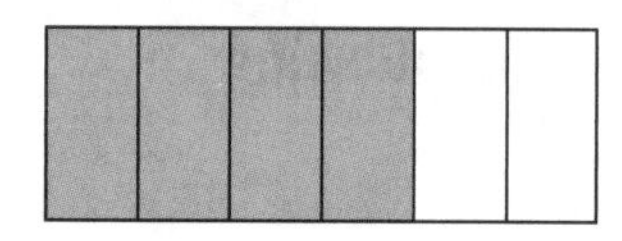

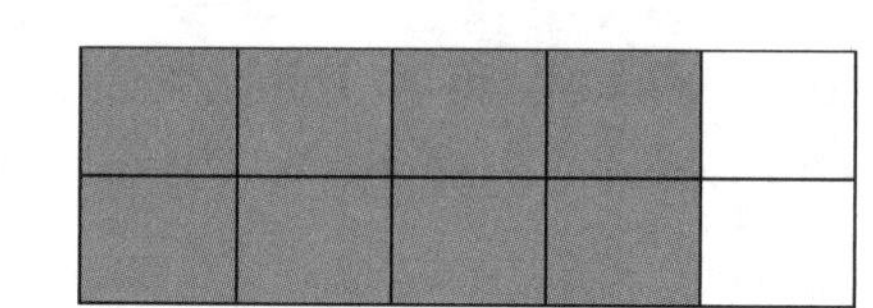

______ ______

# Compare and Order Fractions

**Number lines** can be used to compare and order fractions. On a number line, the fractions become greater as you move from the left to the right.

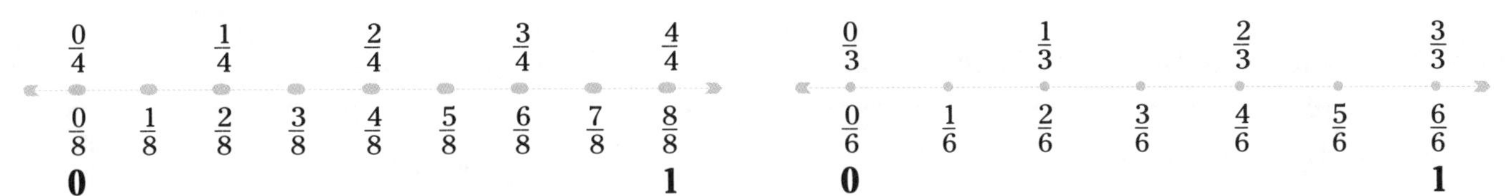


**Compare $\frac{1}{8}$ and $\frac{3}{8}$.**

Find $\frac{1}{8}$ and $\frac{3}{8}$ on the number line. Since $\frac{1}{8}$ is farther to the left, it is less than $\frac{3}{8}$.

$\frac{1}{8} < \frac{3}{8}$

**Compare $\frac{4}{4}$ and $\frac{8}{8}$.**

Find $\frac{4}{4}$ and $\frac{8}{8}$ on the number line. They name the same mark on the line.

$\frac{4}{4} = \frac{8}{8} = 1$

**Compare $\frac{2}{3}$ and $\frac{2}{6}$.**

Find $\frac{2}{3}$ and $\frac{2}{6}$ on the number line. Since $\frac{2}{3}$ is farther to the right, it is greater than $\frac{2}{6}$.

$\frac{2}{3} > \frac{2}{6}$

**Use the number lines above to compare these fractions. Write <, >, or =.**

| | a | b | c | d |
|---|---|---|---|---|
| **1.** | $\frac{7}{8}$ __>__ $\frac{2}{8}$ | $\frac{3}{3}$ ____ $\frac{6}{6}$ | $\frac{3}{6}$ ____ $\frac{5}{6}$ | $\frac{1}{3}$ ____ $\frac{2}{6}$ |
| **2.** | $\frac{1}{4}$ ____ $\frac{2}{4}$ | $\frac{1}{4}$ ____ $\frac{2}{8}$ | $\frac{5}{8}$ ____ $\frac{7}{8}$ | $\frac{1}{6}$ ____ $\frac{2}{3}$ |

**Write the fractions in order from least to greatest.**

| | a | b |
|---|---|---|
| **3.** | $\frac{7}{8}$ $\frac{3}{4}$ $\frac{3}{8}$ ____ $\frac{3}{8}$ $\frac{3}{4}$ $\frac{7}{8}$ | $\frac{1}{3}$ $\frac{3}{6}$ $\frac{1}{6}$ ____ |
| **4.** | $\frac{3}{8}$ $\frac{1}{8}$ $\frac{3}{4}$ ____ | $\frac{2}{3}$ $\frac{1}{3}$ $\frac{3}{6}$ ____ |
| **5.** | $\frac{2}{6}$ $\frac{2}{3}$ $\frac{1}{6}$ ____ | $\frac{7}{8}$ $\frac{1}{4}$ $\frac{4}{8}$ ____ |

# Equivalent Fractions in Higher Terms

To add or subtract fractions, you might need to change a fraction to an equivalent form. To change a fraction to an equivalent fraction in **higher terms**, multiply the numerator and the denominator by the same non-zero number.

**Rewrite $\frac{1}{2}$ with 6 as the denominator.**

| Compare the denominators. | Multiply the numerator and the denominator by 3. |
|---|---|
| $\frac{1}{2} = \frac{\quad}{6}$ **Think:** $2 \times 3 = 6$ | $\frac{1}{2} = \frac{1 \times 3}{2 \times 3} = \frac{3}{6}$ |

**Multiply to write each fraction as an equivalent fraction in higher terms.**

| | *a* | *b* |
|---|---|---|
| **1.** | $\frac{1}{3} = \frac{1 \times 4}{3 \times 4} = \frac{4}{12}$ | $\frac{2}{5} = \frac{2 \times \underline{\quad}}{5 \times \underline{\quad}} = \frac{\quad}{15}$ |
| **2.** | $\frac{3}{8} = \frac{3 \times \underline{\quad}}{8 \times \underline{\quad}} = \frac{\quad}{16}$ | $\frac{2}{3} = \frac{2 \times \underline{\quad}}{3 \times \underline{\quad}} = \frac{\quad}{9}$ |
| **3.** | $\frac{3}{4} = \frac{3 \times \underline{\quad}}{4 \times \underline{\quad}} = \frac{\quad}{12}$ | $\frac{5}{8} = \frac{5 \times \underline{\quad}}{8 \times \underline{\quad}} = \frac{\quad}{16}$ |
| **4.** | $\frac{2}{3} = \frac{2 \times \underline{\quad}}{3 \times \underline{\quad}} = \frac{\quad}{12}$ | $\frac{2}{5} = \frac{2 \times \underline{\quad}}{5 \times \underline{\quad}} = \frac{\quad}{10}$ |

**Write each fraction as an equivalent fraction in higher terms.**

| | *a* | *b* | *c* |
|---|---|---|---|
| **5.** | $\frac{4}{5} = \frac{8}{10}$ | $\frac{1}{4} = \frac{\quad}{12}$ | $\frac{7}{8} = \frac{\quad}{16}$ |
| **6.** | $\frac{1}{3} = \frac{\quad}{15}$ | $\frac{5}{6} = \frac{\quad}{12}$ | $\frac{3}{5} = \frac{\quad}{15}$ |
| **7.** | $\frac{1}{2} = \frac{\quad}{12}$ | $\frac{3}{4} = \frac{\quad}{20}$ | $\frac{3}{10} = \frac{\quad}{20}$ |
| **8.** | $\frac{1}{5} = \frac{\quad}{25}$ | $\frac{2}{3} = \frac{\quad}{15}$ | $\frac{1}{2} = \frac{\quad}{8}$ |
| **9.** | $\frac{1}{2} = \frac{\quad}{10}$ | $\frac{5}{9} = \frac{\quad}{18}$ | $\frac{2}{7} = \frac{\quad}{14}$ |

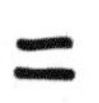

# Equivalent Fractions in Simplest Terms

Sometimes you might need to change a fraction to an equivalent fraction in **simplest terms**. To change a fraction to an equivalent fraction in simplest terms, divide the numerator and denominator by the same greatest number possible.

**Rewrite $\frac{6}{8}$ in simplest terms.**

Consider the numerator and denominator.

$\frac{6}{8} =$ **Think:** 8 can be divided evenly by 4, but 6 cannot.
6 can be divided evenly by 3, but 8 cannot.
Both 8 and 6 can be divided evenly by 2.

Divide the numerator and the denominator by 2.

$\frac{6}{8} = \frac{6 \div 2}{8 \div 2} = \frac{3}{4}$

**A fraction is in simplest terms when 1 is the only number that divides both the numerator and the denominator evenly.**

The fraction $\frac{3}{4}$ is in simplest terms.

**Divide to write each fraction as an equivalent fraction in simplest terms.**

| | a | b | c |
|---|---|---|---|
| 1. | $\frac{5}{15} = \frac{5 \div 5}{15 \div 5} = \frac{1}{3}$ | $\frac{8}{10} = \frac{8 \div \_\_}{10 \div \_\_} =$ | $\frac{9}{12} = \frac{9 \div \_\_}{12 \div \_\_} =$ |
| 2. | $\frac{4}{6} = \frac{4 \div \_\_}{6 \div \_\_} =$ | $\frac{14}{16} = \frac{14 \div \_\_}{16 \div \_\_} =$ | $\frac{10}{25} = \frac{10 \div \_\_}{25 \div \_\_} =$ |
| 3. | $\frac{8}{16} = \frac{8 \div \_\_}{16 \div \_\_} =$ | $\frac{2}{16} = \frac{2 \div \_\_}{16 \div \_\_} =$ | $\frac{2}{4} = \frac{2 \div \_\_}{4 \div \_\_} =$ |

**Write each fraction as an equivalent fraction in simplest terms.**

| | a | b | c |
|---|---|---|---|
| 4. | $\frac{12}{16} = \frac{3}{4}$ | $\frac{2}{6} =$ ______ | $\frac{4}{12} =$ ______ |
| 5. | $\frac{4}{16} =$ ______ | $\frac{6}{10} =$ ______ | $\frac{6}{9} =$ ______ |
| 6. | $\frac{8}{14} =$ ______ | $\frac{5}{25} =$ ______ | $\frac{10}{18} =$ ______ |
| 7. | $\frac{15}{18} =$ ______ | $\frac{3}{12} =$ ______ | $\frac{4}{14} =$ ______ |
| 8. | $\frac{5}{10} =$ ______ | $\frac{8}{18} =$ ______ | $\frac{4}{10} =$ ______ |

# Improper Fractions and Mixed Numbers

An **improper fraction** is a fraction with a numerator that is greater than or equal to the denominator.

**$\frac{4}{4}$, $\frac{14}{2}$, and $\frac{7}{4}$ are improper fractions.**

An improper fraction can be written as a whole or mixed number.

**Write $\frac{4}{4}$ and $\frac{14}{2}$ as whole numbers.**

Divide the numerator by denominator.

$4\overline{)4}$ = 1  $\frac{4}{4} = 1$

$4\overline{)12}$ = 3  $\frac{12}{4} = 3$

**Write $\frac{7}{4}$ as a mixed number.**

Divide the numerator by the denominator. Write the remainder as a fraction by writing the remainder over the divisor.

$4\overline{)7}$ = $1\frac{3}{4}$, $-4$, $3$

$\frac{7}{4} = 1\frac{3}{4}$

A **mixed number** is a whole number and a fraction.

**$2\frac{1}{3}$ is a mixed number.**

A mixed number can be written as an improper fraction.

**Write $2\frac{1}{3}$ as an improper fraction.**

Multiply the whole number and the denominator. Add this product to the numerator. Then write the sum over the denominator.

$2\frac{1}{3} = \frac{2 \times 3 + 1}{3} = \frac{6 + 1}{3} = \frac{7}{3}$

$2\frac{1}{3} = \frac{7}{3}$

**Write as a whole number.**

| | a | b |
|---|---|---|
| 1. | $\frac{20}{5} =$ 4 | $\frac{16}{8} =$ ______ |
| 2. | $\frac{56}{4} =$ ______ | $\frac{14}{14} =$ ______ |

**Write as a mixed number.**

| | | |
|---|---|---|
| 3. | $\frac{13}{12} =$ $1\frac{1}{12}$ | $\frac{18}{7} =$ ______ |
| 4. | $\frac{15}{8} =$ ______ | $\frac{12}{11} =$ ______ |

**Write as an improper fraction.**

| | | |
|---|---|---|
| 5. | $1\frac{4}{5} =$ $\frac{9}{5}$ | $4\frac{3}{7} =$ ______ |
| 6. | $5\frac{1}{4} =$ ______ | $2\frac{2}{5} =$ ______ |

**Write as a mixed number or whole number. Simplify.**

| | a | b | c | d |
|---|---|---|---|---|
| **7.** | $\frac{6}{5}$ = ______ | $\frac{5}{3}$ = ______ | $\frac{32}{6}$ = ______ | $\frac{18}{12}$ = ______ |
| **8.** | $\frac{12}{5}$ = ______ | $\frac{16}{3}$ = ______ | $\frac{12}{9}$ = ______ | $\frac{19}{4}$ = ______ |
| **9.** | $\frac{21}{12}$ = ______ | $\frac{23}{6}$ = ______ | $\frac{13}{2}$ = ______ | $\frac{20}{8}$ = ______ |
| **10.** | $\frac{36}{9}$ = ______ | $\frac{12}{12}$ = ______ | $\frac{16}{8}$ = ______ | $\frac{54}{6}$ = ______ |

**Write as an improper fraction.**

| | a | b | c | d |
|---|---|---|---|---|
| **11.** | $4\frac{1}{4}$ = ______ | $3\frac{2}{3}$ = ______ | $4\frac{1}{2}$ = ______ | $1\frac{1}{6}$ = ______ |
| **12.** | $2\frac{1}{4}$ = ______ | $1\frac{7}{8}$ = ______ | $4\frac{1}{3}$ = ______ | $3\frac{4}{5}$ = ______ |
| **13.** | $4\frac{2}{3}$ = ______ | $1\frac{1}{10}$ = ______ | $2\frac{3}{5}$ = ______ | $2\frac{5}{7}$ = ______ |
| **14.** | $2\frac{2}{9}$ = ______ | $4\frac{2}{5}$ = ______ | $5\frac{1}{2}$ = ______ | $4\frac{1}{6}$ = ______ |

## Addition and Subtraction of Fractions with Like Denominators

To add or subtract fractions with like denominators, add or subtract the numerators. Use the same denominator. Simplify the answer.

**Remember,**

- to simplify an improper fraction, write it as a whole number or a mixed number.
- to simplify a proper fraction, write it in simplest terms.

**Find:** $\frac{4}{5} + \frac{3}{5}$

Add the numerators.

$$\frac{3}{5} + \frac{4}{5} = 7$$

Use the same denominator.

$$\frac{3}{5} + \frac{4}{5} = \frac{7}{5} = 1\frac{2}{5}$$

Simplify the answer.

**Find:** $\frac{7}{8} - \frac{3}{8}$

Subtract the numerators.

$$\frac{7}{8} - \frac{3}{8} = 4$$

Use the same denominator.

$$\frac{7}{8} - \frac{3}{8} = \frac{4}{8} = \frac{1}{2}$$

Simplify the answer.

**Add. Simplify.**

| | a | b | c | d | e |
|---|---|---|---|---|---|
| **1.** | $\frac{5}{12} + \frac{3}{12} = \frac{8}{12} = \frac{2}{3}$ | $\frac{4}{9} + \frac{2}{9}$ | $\frac{3}{7} + \frac{1}{7}$ | $\frac{3}{8} + \frac{1}{8}$ | $\frac{4}{9} + \frac{3}{9}$ |
| **2.** | $\frac{3}{5} + \frac{3}{5}$ | $\frac{4}{5} + \frac{3}{5}$ | $\frac{3}{8} + \frac{6}{8}$ | $\frac{2}{3} + \frac{2}{3}$ | $\frac{7}{8} + \frac{1}{8}$ |

**Subtract. Simplify.**

| | a | b | c | d | e |
|---|---|---|---|---|---|
| **3.** | $\frac{5}{8} - \frac{1}{8} = \frac{4}{8} = \frac{1}{2}$ | $\frac{6}{6} - \frac{4}{6}$ | $\frac{5}{8} - \frac{3}{8}$ | $\frac{5}{6} - \frac{2}{6}$ | $\frac{5}{9} - \frac{2}{9}$ |

## Addition and Subtraction of Mixed Numbers with Like Denominators

To add or subtract mixed numbers with like denominators, first add or subtract the fractions. Then add or subtract the whole numbers and simplify.

**Find:** $1\frac{1}{8} + 2\frac{5}{8}$

| Add the fractions. | Add the whole numbers. Simplify. |
|---|---|
| $1\frac{1}{8}$ | $1\frac{1}{8}$ |
| $+2\frac{5}{8}$ | $+2\frac{5}{8}$ |
| $\frac{6}{8}$ | $3\frac{6}{8} = 3\frac{3}{4}$ |

**Find:** $8\frac{5}{9} - 4\frac{2}{9}$

| Subtract the fractions. | Subtract the whole numbers. Simplify. |
|---|---|
| $8\frac{5}{9}$ | $8\frac{5}{9}$ |
| $-4\frac{2}{9}$ | $-4\frac{2}{9}$ |
| $\frac{3}{9}$ | $4\frac{3}{9} = 4\frac{1}{3}$ |

**Add. Simplify.**

| | a | b | c | d | e |
|---|---|---|---|---|---|
| **1.** | $2\frac{1}{4} + 3\frac{1}{4}$ | $3\frac{2}{4} + 6\frac{1}{4}$ | $9\frac{3}{5} + 5\frac{1}{5}$ | $6\frac{1}{8} + 2\frac{3}{8}$ | $4\frac{3}{10} + 5\frac{3}{10}$ |
| | $5\frac{2}{4} = 5\frac{1}{2}$ | | | | |
| **2.** | $8\frac{1}{5} + 9\frac{3}{5}$ | $6\frac{1}{4} + 9\frac{2}{4}$ | $6\frac{1}{3} + 5\frac{1}{3}$ | $12\frac{2}{5} + 9\frac{1}{5}$ | $12\frac{2}{9} + 4\frac{4}{9}$ |

**Subtract. Simplify.**

| | a | b | c | d | e |
|---|---|---|---|---|---|
| **3.** | $4\frac{11}{12} - 2\frac{1}{12}$ | $3\frac{7}{8} - 2\frac{3}{8}$ | $6\frac{7}{12} - 2\frac{5}{12}$ | $5\frac{9}{10} - 3\frac{7}{10}$ | $7\frac{5}{6} - 2\frac{1}{6}$ |
| | $2\frac{10}{12} = 2\frac{5}{6}$ | | | | |
| **4.** | $7\frac{6}{8} - 4\frac{4}{8}$ | $6\frac{3}{8} - 1\frac{1}{8}$ | $8\frac{4}{5} - 3\frac{2}{5}$ | $5\frac{5}{12} - 4\frac{1}{12}$ | $8\frac{7}{10} - 4\frac{3}{10}$ |

## Problem-Solving Method: Use Logic

*Recycling Times* reported the aluminum can recycling statistics for 1990, 1995, and 1999. In those years, $\frac{3}{5}$, $\frac{2}{3}$, and $\frac{3}{7}$ of all the cans collected were recycled. The fraction for 1999 has an even numerator. More cans were recycled in 1995 than in 1990. What were the aluminum can recycling statistics for 1990, 1995, and 1999?

**Understand the problem.**

- **What do you want to know?**
  the can recycling statistics for 1990, 1995, and 1999

- **What information are you given?**
  In those years, $\frac{3}{5}$, $\frac{2}{3}$, and $\frac{3}{7}$ of all the cans collected were recycled.

  **Clue 1:** The fraction for 1999 has an even numerator.
  **Clue 2:** More cans were recycled in 1995 than in 1990.

**Plan how to solve it.**

- **What method can you use?**
  You can organize all the possibilities in a table.
  Then you can use logic to match the clues to the possibilities.

**Solve it.**

- **How can you use this method to solve the problem?**
  Since each of the years has one statistic, there can only be one YES in each row and column. You can use a number line to compare the fractions for 1995 and 1990.

| | $\frac{3}{5}$ | $\frac{2}{3}$ | $\frac{3}{7}$ |
|---|---|---|---|
| 1990 | no | no | **YES** |
| 1995 | **YES** | no | no |
| 1999 | no | **YES** | no |

- **What is the answer?**

  In 1990, $\frac{3}{7}$ of all the aluminum cans were recycled.
  In 1995, $\frac{3}{5}$ of all the aluminum cans were recycled.
  In 1999, $\frac{2}{3}$ of all the aluminum cans were recycled.

**Check:**
In $\frac{2}{3}$, 2 is even.
$\frac{3}{5} > \frac{3}{7}$

**Look back and check your answer.**

- **Is your answer reasonable?**

  **Clue 1:** The fraction for 1999 has an even numerator.
  **Clue 2:** More cans were recycled in 1995 than in 1990.

  The answer matches the clues.
  The answer is reasonable.

**Use logic to solve each problem.**

1. In 1998, New York, Cleveland, and Boston had the best records in American League baseball. They won $\frac{7}{10}$, $\frac{5}{9}$, and $\frac{1}{2}$ of their games. New York had the best record. Cleveland won fewer games than Boston. What fraction of their games did each team win?

New York ____________

Cleveland ____________

Boston ____________

2. In the United States, petroleum, natural gas, and coal are used more than any other sources of energy. They make up $\frac{1}{5}$, $\frac{1}{4}$, and $\frac{2}{5}$ of all the energy used. Coal is used the least. More petroleum is used than natural gas. What fraction is each energy source?

petroleum ____________

natural gas ____________

coal ____________

3. The smallest mammal in the world is a Kitti's hognosed bat. The next two smallest bats are the proboscis bat and the banana bat. Their weights are $\frac{11}{10}$, $\frac{7}{10}$, and $\frac{9}{10}$ of an ounce. The banana bat weighs less than the proboscis bat. What are the weights of the three smallest bats?

Kitti's hognosed bat ____________

proboscis bat ____________

banana bat ____________

# Estimate Fractions

Use these rules to **round** fractions.

| When the numerator is: | Round to: |
|---|---|
| much less than the denominator | 0 |
| about $\frac{1}{2}$ the denominator | $\frac{1}{2}$ |
| about the same as the denominator | 1 |

To **estimate** fraction sums or differences, round the fractions. Then add or subtract.

**Find:** $\frac{3}{8} + \frac{1}{5}$

Round the fractions.

$\frac{3}{8} \rightarrow \frac{1}{2}$

$+\frac{1}{5} \rightarrow +0$

Add.

$\frac{1}{2} + 0 = \frac{1}{2}$

**Round the fractions. Write *about 0*, *about* $\frac{1}{2}$, or *about 1*.**

| | a | b |
|---|---|---|
| 1. | $\frac{6}{10}$ about $\frac{1}{2}$ | $\frac{3}{4}$ about 1 |
| 2. | $\frac{1}{7}$ about 0 | $\frac{2}{11}$ about 0 |
| 3. | $\frac{7}{8}$ about 1 | $\frac{5}{9}$ about half |

**Estimate the sums or differences.**

| | a | b | c |
|---|---|---|---|
| 4. | $\frac{6}{7} \rightarrow 1$<br>$-\frac{1}{10} \rightarrow -0$<br>$1$ | $\frac{4}{9} \rightarrow$<br>$+\frac{4}{7} \rightarrow$ | $\frac{1}{6} \rightarrow$<br>$+\frac{7}{8} \rightarrow$ |
| 5. | $\frac{5}{6} \rightarrow$<br>$-\frac{2}{3} \rightarrow$ | $\frac{11}{12} \rightarrow$<br>$-\frac{1}{9} \rightarrow$ | $\frac{3}{5} \rightarrow$<br>$+\frac{1}{6} \rightarrow$ |
| 6. | $\frac{1}{4} \rightarrow$<br>$+\frac{6}{7} \rightarrow$ | $\frac{7}{8} \rightarrow$<br>$-\frac{4}{9} \rightarrow$ | $\frac{5}{9} \rightarrow$<br>$+\frac{2}{5} \rightarrow$ |

# Addition of Fractions with Different Denominators

To add fractions with different denominators, first rewrite the fractions as equivalent fractions with like denominators. Then add and simplify the answer.

**Find:** $\frac{1}{3} + \frac{5}{6}$

Write equivalent fractions with like denominators.

$$\frac{1}{3} = \frac{2}{6}$$
$$+\frac{5}{6} = \frac{5}{6}$$

**Remember:** $\frac{1}{3} = \frac{1 \times 2}{3 \times 2} = \frac{2}{6}$

Add the numerators. Use the same denominator.

$$\frac{1}{3} = \frac{2}{6}$$
$$+\frac{5}{6} = \frac{5}{6}$$
$$\frac{7}{6} = 1\frac{1}{6}$$

Simplify the answer.

**Add. Simplify.**

| | a | b | c | d |
|---|---|---|---|---|
| **1.** | $\frac{1}{6} = \frac{1}{6}$ <br> $+\frac{1}{3} = \frac{2}{6}$ <br> $\frac{3}{6} = \frac{1}{2}$ | $\frac{3}{10} = \frac{3}{10}$ <br> $+\frac{1}{2} = \frac{5}{10}$ <br> $\frac{8}{10}$ | $\frac{1}{8} = \frac{}{8}$ <br> $+\frac{3}{4} = \frac{}{8}$ | $\frac{1}{2} = \frac{}{6}$ <br> $+\frac{1}{6} = \frac{}{6}$ |
| **2.** | $\frac{3}{5} = \frac{}{10}$ <br> $+\frac{7}{10} = \frac{}{10}$ | $\frac{6}{7} = \frac{}{14}$ <br> $+\frac{5}{14} = \frac{}{14}$ | $\frac{8}{9} = \frac{}{9}$ <br> $+\frac{2}{3} = \frac{}{9}$ | $\frac{10}{12} = \frac{10}{12}$ <br> $+\frac{3}{4} = \frac{9}{12}$ <br> $1\frac{7}{12}$ |
| **3.** | $\frac{1}{8}$ <br> $+\frac{1}{4}$ | $\frac{1}{5}$ <br> $+\frac{3}{10}$ | $\frac{3}{10}$ <br> $+\frac{1}{2}$ | $\frac{3}{4}$ <br> $+\frac{1}{8}$ |

## Subtraction of Fractions with Different Denominators

To subtract fractions with different denominators, first rewrite the fractions as equivalent fractions with like denominators. Then subtract and simplify the answer.

**Find:** $\frac{9}{10} - \frac{1}{2}$

Write equivalent fractions with like denominators.

$$\begin{array}{r} \frac{9}{10} = \frac{9}{10} \\ -\frac{1}{2} = \frac{5}{10} \\ \hline \end{array}$$

**Remember:** $\frac{1}{2} = \frac{1 \times 5}{2 \times 5} = \frac{5}{10}$

Subtract the numerators. Use the same denominator.

$$\begin{array}{r} \frac{9}{10} = \frac{9}{10} \\ -\frac{1}{2} = \frac{5}{10} \\ \hline \frac{4}{10} = \frac{2}{5} \end{array}$$

Simplify the answer.

**Subtract. Simplify.**

| | a | b | c | d |
|---|---|---|---|---|
| 1. | $\frac{1}{2} = \frac{4}{8}$<br>$-\frac{1}{8} = \frac{1}{8}$<br>$\frac{3}{8}$ | $\frac{1}{3} = \frac{\phantom{0}}{6}$<br>$-\frac{1}{6} = \frac{\phantom{0}}{6}$ | $\frac{3}{4} = \frac{\phantom{0}}{4}$<br>$-\frac{1}{2} = \frac{\phantom{0}}{4}$ | $\frac{5}{6} = \frac{\phantom{0}}{6}$<br>$-\frac{2}{3} = \frac{\phantom{0}}{6}$ |
| 2. | $\frac{13}{14} = \frac{\phantom{0}}{14}$<br>$-\frac{3}{7} = \frac{\phantom{0}}{14}$ | $\frac{1}{2} = \frac{\phantom{0}}{6}$<br>$-\frac{1}{6} = \frac{\phantom{0}}{6}$ | $\frac{4}{5} = \frac{\phantom{0}}{10}$<br>$-\frac{3}{10} = \frac{\phantom{0}}{10}$ | $\frac{7}{20} = \frac{\phantom{0}}{20}$<br>$-\frac{1}{4} = \frac{\phantom{0}}{20}$ |

# Addition of Mixed Numbers with Different Denominators

To add mixed numbers with different denominators, write the mixed numbers with like denominators. Add the fractions. Then add the whole numbers and simplify.

**Find:** $3\frac{5}{12} + 5\frac{1}{3}$

Write the mixed numbers with like denominators.

$$\begin{array}{r} 3\frac{5}{12} = 3\frac{5}{12} \\ +5\frac{1}{3} = 5\frac{4}{12} \\ \hline \end{array}$$

Add the fractions.

$$\begin{array}{r} 3\frac{5}{12} = 3\frac{5}{12} \\ +5\frac{1}{3} = 5\frac{4}{12} \\ \hline \frac{9}{12} \end{array}$$

Add the whole numbers.

$$\begin{array}{r} 3\frac{5}{12} = 3\frac{5}{12} \\ +5\frac{1}{3} = 5\frac{4}{12} \\ \hline 8\frac{9}{12} \end{array}$$

Simplify.

$8\frac{9}{12} = 8\frac{3}{4}$

**Remember:** $5\frac{1}{3} = 5\frac{4}{12}$
They are equivalent fractions.

**Add. Simplify.**

| | a | b | c | d |
|---|---|---|---|---|
| **1.** | $\begin{array}{r} 3\frac{1}{8} = 3\frac{1}{8} \\ +6\frac{3}{4} = 6\frac{6}{8} \\ \hline 9\frac{7}{8} \end{array}$ | $\begin{array}{r} 9\frac{2}{3} = 9\frac{}{6} \\ +1\frac{1}{6} = 1\frac{1}{6} \\ \hline \end{array}$ | $\begin{array}{r} 4\frac{1}{2} = 4\frac{}{12} \\ +1\frac{5}{12} = 1\frac{5}{12} \\ \hline \end{array}$ | $\begin{array}{r} 2\frac{5}{8} = 2\frac{5}{8} \\ +6\frac{1}{4} = 6\frac{}{8} \\ \hline \end{array}$ |
| **2.** | $\begin{array}{r} 12\frac{3}{4} = \\ +4\frac{1}{8} = \\ \hline \end{array}$ | $\begin{array}{r} 5\frac{3}{8} = \\ +15\frac{1}{2} = \\ \hline \end{array}$ | $\begin{array}{r} 8\frac{2}{3} = \\ +3\frac{1}{9} = \\ \hline \end{array}$ | $\begin{array}{r} 7\frac{1}{10} = \\ +6\frac{3}{5} = \\ \hline \end{array}$ |
| **3.** | $\begin{array}{r} 5\frac{5}{8} = \\ +4\frac{1}{4} = \\ \hline \end{array}$ | $\begin{array}{r} 15\frac{5}{12} = \\ +8\frac{1}{3} = \\ \hline \end{array}$ | $\begin{array}{r} 6\frac{3}{10} = \\ +10\frac{1}{5} = \\ \hline \end{array}$ | $\begin{array}{r} 9\frac{2}{3} = \\ +8\frac{2}{9} = \\ \hline \end{array}$ |

## Addition of Mixed Numbers with Regrouping

When adding mixed numbers, sometimes your sum will contain an improper fraction. To regroup a sum that contains an improper fraction, first write the improper fraction as a mixed number. Then add and simplify.

**Find:** $6\frac{2}{3} + 2\frac{5}{6}$

Write the fractions with like denominators. Add the mixed numbers.

$$6\frac{2}{3} = 6\frac{4}{6}$$
$$+2\frac{5}{6} = 2\frac{5}{6}$$
$$8\frac{9}{6}$$

The sum, $8\frac{9}{6}$, contains an improper fraction. To regroup, write the improper fraction as a mixed number.

$$\frac{9}{6} = 1\frac{3}{6}$$

Then add the whole numbers.

$$8\frac{9}{6} = 8 + 1\frac{3}{6} = 9\frac{3}{6}$$

Simplify.

$$9\frac{3}{6} = 9\frac{1}{2}$$

**Regroup. Simplify.**

| | a | b | c | d |
|---|---|---|---|---|
| **1.** | $3\frac{5}{3}$   $\frac{5}{3} = 1\frac{2}{3}$   $3 + 1\frac{2}{3} = 4\frac{2}{3}$ | $6\frac{13}{10}$ | $9\frac{9}{8}$ | $12\frac{7}{4}$ |
| **2.** | $4\frac{8}{6}$ | $8\frac{12}{9}$ | $7\frac{18}{12}$ | $10\frac{14}{8}$ |

**Add. Regroup. Simplify.**

a b c

**3.** $2\frac{3}{4} = 2\frac{3}{4}$, $+1\frac{1}{2} = 1\frac{2}{4}$, $3\frac{5}{4} = 3 + 1\frac{1}{4} = 4\frac{1}{4}$    $4\frac{5}{8} =$, $+2\frac{3}{4} =$    $5\frac{9}{10} =$, $+3\frac{2}{5} =$

**4.** $4\frac{2}{3} =$, $+8\frac{7}{12} =$    $3\frac{7}{10} =$, $+3\frac{4}{5} =$    $6\frac{11}{18} =$, $+2\frac{5}{9} =$

# Subtraction of Mixed Numbers with Different Denominators

To subtract mixed numbers with different denominators, write the mixed numbers with like denominators. Subtract the fractions. Subtract the whole numbers. Simplify.

**Find:** $9\frac{11}{12} - 2\frac{1}{4}$

| Write the mixed numbers with like denominators. | Subtract the fractions. | Subtract the whole numbers. | Simplify. |
|---|---|---|---|
| $9\frac{11}{12} = 9\frac{11}{12}$<br>$-2\frac{1}{4} = 2\frac{3}{12}$ | $9\frac{11}{12} = 9\frac{11}{12}$<br>$-2\frac{1}{4} = 2\frac{3}{12}$<br>$\frac{8}{12}$ | $9\frac{11}{12} = 9\frac{11}{12}$<br>$-2\frac{1}{4} = 2\frac{3}{12}$<br>$7\frac{8}{12}$ | $7\frac{8}{12} = 7\frac{2}{3}$ |

**Subtract. Simplify.**

| | a | b | c | d |
|---|---|---|---|---|
| **1.** | $8\frac{5}{6} = 8\frac{5}{6}$<br>$-2\frac{1}{3} = 2\frac{2}{6}$<br>$6\frac{3}{6} = 6\frac{1}{2}$ | $5\frac{3}{4} = 5\frac{3}{4}$<br>$-3\frac{1}{2} = 3\frac{\phantom{0}}{4}$ | $9\frac{5}{8} = 9\frac{5}{8}$<br>$-3\frac{1}{4} = 3\frac{\phantom{0}}{8}$ | $8\frac{7}{10} = 8\frac{7}{10}$<br>$-1\frac{1}{2} = 1\frac{\phantom{0}}{10}$ |
| **2.** | $15\frac{3}{4} =$<br>$-\ 8\frac{3}{8} =$ | $16\frac{5}{6} =$<br>$-10\frac{1}{2} =$ | $9\frac{5}{6} =$<br>$-6\frac{2}{3} =$ | $12\frac{5}{8} =$<br>$-\ 7\frac{1}{4} =$ |
| **3.** | $3\frac{4}{9} =$<br>$-1\frac{1}{3} =$ | $5\frac{6}{7} =$<br>$-2\frac{1}{14} =$ | $4\frac{5}{12} =$<br>$-3\frac{1}{4} =$ | $9\frac{7}{18} =$<br>$-6\frac{2}{9} =$ |

## Subtraction of Fractions and Mixed Numbers from Whole Numbers

Sometimes you will need to subtract a fraction from a whole number.
To subtract from a whole number, write the whole number as a mixed number with a like denominator. Then subtract the fractions. Subtract the whole numbers.

**Find:** $6 - 4\frac{2}{3}$

| To subtract, you need two fractions with like denominators. | Write 6 as a mixed number with 3 as the denominator. | Subtract the fractions. | Subtract the whole numbers. |
|---|---|---|---|
| $6$ <br> $-4\frac{2}{3}$ | $6 = 5 + \frac{3}{3} = 5\frac{3}{3}$ <br> Remember: $\frac{3}{3} = 1$ | $6 = 5\frac{3}{3}$ <br> $-4\frac{2}{3} = 4\frac{2}{3}$ <br> $\frac{1}{3}$ | $6 = 5\frac{3}{3}$ <br> $-4\frac{2}{3} = 4\frac{2}{3}$ <br> $1\frac{1}{3}$ |

**Write each whole number as a mixed number.**

| | a | b | c |
|---|---|---|---|
| 1. | $4 = 3 + \frac{6}{6} = 3\frac{6}{6}$ | $6 = 5 + \frac{}{8} =$ | $2 = 1 + \frac{}{3} =$ |
| 2. | $10 = 9 + \frac{}{5} =$ | $14 = 13 + \frac{}{3} =$ | $9 = 8 + \frac{}{6} =$ |

**Subtract.**

| | a | b | c | d |
|---|---|---|---|---|
| 3. | $9 = 8\frac{4}{4}$ <br> $-2\frac{3}{4} = 2\frac{3}{4}$ <br> $6\frac{1}{4}$ | $12 = 11\frac{}{3}$ <br> $-5\frac{1}{3} = 5\frac{1}{3}$ | $9 = 8\frac{}{4}$ <br> $-3\frac{1}{4} = 3\frac{1}{4}$ | $20 = 19\frac{}{10}$ <br> $-3\frac{7}{10} = 3\frac{7}{10}$ |
| 4. | $17 =$ <br> $-5\frac{2}{15} =$ | $5 =$ <br> $-\frac{1}{6} =$ | $13 =$ <br> $-\frac{4}{9} =$ | $9 =$ <br> $-\frac{3}{7} =$ |

# Subtraction of Mixed Numbers with Regrouping

When subtracting mixed numbers, it may be necessary to regroup first. To regroup a mixed number for subtraction, write the whole number part as a mixed number. Add the mixed number and the fraction. Then subtract and simplify.

**Find:** $6\frac{5}{12} - 2\frac{3}{4}$

Write the fractions with like denominators. Compare the numerators.

$$\begin{array}{r} 6\frac{5}{12} = 6\frac{5}{12} \\ -2\frac{3}{4} = 2\frac{9}{12} \\ \hline \end{array}$$

$\frac{9}{12}$ is greater than $\frac{5}{12}$. You can't subtract the fractions.

To regroup $6\frac{5}{12}$, write 6 as a mixed number.

$6 = 5\frac{12}{12}$

Add the mixed number and the fraction.

$6\frac{5}{12} = 5\frac{12}{12} + \frac{5}{12} = 5\frac{17}{12}$

**Note:** $\frac{17}{12}$ is an improper fraction.

Subtract and simplify.

$$\begin{array}{r} 6\frac{5}{12} = 5\frac{17}{12} \\ -2\frac{3}{4} = 2\frac{9}{12} \\ \hline 3\frac{8}{12} = 3\frac{2}{3} \end{array}$$

**Regroup each mixed number.**

| | a | b | c |
|---|---|---|---|
| 1. | $6\frac{1}{3} = 5\frac{3}{3} + \frac{1}{3} = 5\frac{4}{3}$ | $8\frac{7}{8} = 7\frac{\phantom{0}}{8}$ | $9\frac{1}{6} = 8\frac{\phantom{0}}{6}$ |
| 2. | $3\frac{6}{8} = 2\frac{\phantom{0}}{8}$ | $5\frac{9}{12} = 4\frac{\phantom{0}}{12}$ | $14\frac{8}{10} = 13\frac{\phantom{0}}{10}$ |

**Regroup. Subtract. Simplify.**

| | a | b | c |
|---|---|---|---|
| 3. | $\begin{array}{r} 9\frac{3}{8} = 9\frac{3}{8} = 8\frac{11}{8} \\ -4\frac{3}{4} = 4\frac{6}{8} = 4\frac{6}{8} \\ \hline 4\frac{5}{8} \end{array}$ | $\begin{array}{r} 7\frac{1}{3} = 7\frac{\phantom{0}}{6} \\ -2\frac{5}{6} = 2\frac{5}{6} \\ \hline \end{array}$ | $\begin{array}{r} 9\frac{1}{5} = 9\frac{\phantom{0}}{10} \\ -2\frac{3}{10} = 2\frac{3}{10} \\ \hline \end{array}$ |
| 4. | $\begin{array}{r} 6\frac{3}{10} \\ -4\frac{2}{5} \\ \hline \end{array}$ | $\begin{array}{r} 13\frac{1}{4} \\ -6\frac{5}{8} \\ \hline \end{array}$ | $\begin{array}{r} 12\frac{5}{12} \\ -7\frac{2}{3} \\ \hline \end{array}$ |

## Problem-Solving Method: Make a Model

Brent sewed two pieces of cloth end to end to make a flag. The first piece was yellow and $\frac{1}{2}$ yard long. The second piece was $\frac{1}{3}$ yard long and blue. How long was the flag that Brent sewed?

**Understand the problem.**

- **What do you want to know?**
  the length of the flag

- **What information is given?**
  He sewed $\frac{1}{2}$ yard of yellow cloth to $\frac{1}{3}$ yard of blue cloth.

**Plan how to solve it.**

- **What method can you use?**
  You can make a model of the flag.

**Solve it.**

- **How can you use this method to solve the problem?**
  Use fraction strips to model the sum of $\frac{1}{2}$ yard and $\frac{1}{3}$ yard.

Place one $\frac{1}{2}$ strip and one $\frac{1}{3}$ strip end to end under a 1-whole fraction strip.

| 1 | |
|---|---|
| $\frac{1}{2}$ | $\frac{1}{3}$ |

Find equal size fraction strips that fit exactly under $\frac{1}{2}$ and $\frac{1}{3}$.

| 1 | | | | |
|---|---|---|---|---|
| $\frac{1}{2}$ | | | $\frac{1}{3}$ | |
| $\frac{1}{6}$ | $\frac{1}{6}$ | $\frac{1}{6}$ | $\frac{1}{6}$ | $\frac{1}{6}$ |

- **What is the answer?**
  The flag was $\frac{5}{6}$ yard long.

**Look back and check your answer.**

- **Is your answer reasonable?**
  You can check your model with addition.

$$\begin{array}{r} \frac{1}{2} = \frac{3}{6} \\ +\frac{1}{3} = \frac{2}{6} \\ \hline \frac{5}{6} \end{array}$$

The model and the sum are the same.
The answer is reasonable.

**Make a model to solve each problem.**

1. Kendra walked $\frac{1}{4}$ mile from school to the store. Then she walked $\frac{2}{3}$ mile from the store to home. How far did Kendra walk in all?

| 1 | | | | | | | | | | | |
|---|---|---|---|---|---|---|---|---|---|---|---|
| $\frac{1}{4}$ | | | $\frac{1}{3}$ | | | | $\frac{1}{3}$ | | | | |
| $\frac{1}{12}$ | $\frac{1}{12}$ | $\frac{1}{12}$ | $\frac{1}{12}$ | $\frac{1}{12}$ | $\frac{1}{12}$ | $\frac{1}{12}$ | $\frac{1}{12}$ | $\frac{1}{12}$ | $\frac{1}{12}$ | $\frac{1}{12}$ | |

Answer ______________________

2. Jack grew $\frac{1}{2}$ inch in May and $\frac{2}{5}$ inch in June. How many inches did he grow in the two months altogether?

Answer ______________________

3. An average bark beetle is $\frac{1}{8}$ inch long. Carpenter ants are usually $\frac{1}{2}$ inch longer than a bark beetle. How long is an average carpenter ant?

Answer ______________________

4. Amy used $\frac{1}{4}$ yard of lace for curtains. Then she used $\frac{1}{3}$ yard of lace for a table cloth. How many yards of lace did Amy use in all?

Answer ______________________

5. José used $\frac{1}{2}$ cup of white flour and $\frac{1}{4}$ cup of whole-wheat flour to make bread. How much flour did he use in all?

Answer ______________________

## Problem Solving

**Solve. Simplify.**

**1.** Ruby and Chung work together. Ruby lives $13\frac{1}{2}$ miles from work. Chung lives $2\frac{1}{6}$ miles beyond Ruby. How far from work does Chung live?

Answer ______________________

**2.** Anne is $64\frac{1}{2}$ inches tall. Shaneeka is $61\frac{1}{4}$ inches tall. How much taller is Anne than Shaneeka?

Answer ______________________

**3.** Fred used $1\frac{1}{6}$ cups of raisins and $3\frac{1}{3}$ cups of nuts to make his trail mix. How many cups of the mix did he make?

Answer ______________________

**4.** The world's biggest pineapple weighed $17\frac{3}{4}$ pounds. The world's biggest apple weighed $3\frac{11}{16}$ pounds. How much more did the pineapple weigh than the apple?

Answer ______________________

**5.** The largest butterfly in North America is the giant swallowtail. Its wingspan is 5 inches wide. The smallest is the pygmy blue. Its wingspan is only $\frac{1}{2}$ inch. How much larger is a giant swallowtail than a pygmy blue?

Answer ______________________

**6.** An average car uses $1\frac{3}{5}$ ounces of gasoline for one minute of sitting still with the engine on. If a car waits at a traffic light for 2 minutes, how much gasoline will it use?

Answer ______________________

**7.** Inez caught two fish. One weighed $3\frac{1}{2}$ pounds. The second fish weighed $4\frac{1}{4}$ pounds. How many pounds of fish did she catch?

Answer ______________________

# UNIT 4 Review

**Write the fraction for the word name.**

| | a | b | c |
|---|---|---|---|
| 1. | three-fifths ______ | four-ninths ______ | one-sixth ______ |

**Write the fractions in order from least to greatest.**

| | a | b |
|---|---|---|
| 2. | $\frac{3}{9}$ $\frac{2}{3}$ $\frac{1}{9}$ ______ | $\frac{4}{5}$ $\frac{3}{10}$ $\frac{3}{5}$ ______ |

**Write each fraction as an equivalent fraction in simplest terms.**

| | a | b | c | d |
|---|---|---|---|---|
| 3. | $\frac{9}{12} =$ ______ | $\frac{6}{10} =$ ______ | $\frac{4}{6} =$ ______ | $\frac{4}{8} =$ ______ |

**Rewrite each fraction as an equivalent fraction in higher terms.**

| | a | b | c | d |
|---|---|---|---|---|
| 4. | $\frac{2}{3} = \frac{\phantom{0}}{9}$ | $\frac{1}{6} = \frac{\phantom{0}}{12}$ | $\frac{3}{5} = \frac{\phantom{0}}{15}$ | $\frac{1}{2} = \frac{\phantom{0}}{10}$ |

**Add. Simplify.**

| | a | b | c | d |
|---|---|---|---|---|
| 5. | $\frac{3}{9} + \frac{4}{9}$ | $\frac{4}{7} + \frac{3}{7}$ | $\frac{1}{8} + \frac{4}{8}$ | $\frac{3}{10} + \frac{3}{10}$ |
| 6. | $\frac{3}{8} + \frac{1}{4}$ | $\frac{1}{3} + \frac{7}{9}$ | $\frac{3}{5} + \frac{3}{10}$ | $\frac{1}{2} + \frac{1}{16}$ |
| 7. | $7\frac{1}{3} + 3\frac{4}{9}$ | $6\frac{3}{4} + 4\frac{5}{12}$ | $9\frac{1}{2} + 1\frac{3}{8}$ | $5\frac{1}{5} + 2\frac{4}{15}$ |

# UNIT 4 Review

**Write as a mixed number or whole number.**

| | a | b | c | d |
|---|---|---|---|---|
| **8.** | $\frac{31}{8}$ = ________ | $\frac{13}{6}$ = ________ | $\frac{25}{5}$ = ________ | $\frac{19}{4}$ = ________ |

**Write as an improper fraction.**

| | a | b | c | d |
|---|---|---|---|---|
| **9.** | $4\frac{1}{3}$ = ________ | $8\frac{2}{5}$ = ________ | $2\frac{1}{8}$ = ________ | $5\frac{3}{10}$ = ________ |

**Write each whole number as a mixed number.**

| | a | b | c | d |
|---|---|---|---|---|
| **10.** | $5 = 4 + \frac{}{2} =$ | $8 = 7 + \frac{5}{} =$ | $12 = 11 + \frac{}{9} =$ | $16 = 15 + \frac{7}{} =$ |

**Subtract. Simplify.**

| | a | b | c | d |
|---|---|---|---|---|
| **11.** | $\frac{7}{10} - \frac{3}{10}$ | $\frac{4}{7} - \frac{2}{7}$ | $\frac{11}{12} - \frac{7}{12}$ | $\frac{5}{6} - \frac{2}{6}$ |
| **12.** | $7\frac{2}{3} - 2\frac{1}{3}$ | $5\frac{5}{6} - 3\frac{1}{6}$ | $8\frac{9}{10} - 4\frac{3}{10}$ | $9\frac{7}{8} - 1\frac{1}{8}$ |
| **13.** | $9\frac{1}{6} - 3\frac{2}{3}$ | $6\frac{1}{2} - 4\frac{3}{4}$ | $5\frac{1}{5} - 1\frac{3}{10}$ | $8 - 3\frac{4}{9}$ |

**Estimate the sums or differences.**

| | a | b | c |
|---|---|---|---|
| **14.** | $\frac{1}{5} \rightarrow$ <br> $+\frac{4}{9} \rightarrow$ | $\frac{7}{8} \rightarrow$ <br> $-\frac{1}{3} \rightarrow$ | $\frac{3}{10} \rightarrow$ <br> $+\frac{4}{5} \rightarrow$ |

**Use logic to solve each problem.**

**15.** In 1998, Atlanta, Philadelphia, and New York had the best records in the Eastern division of National League baseball. They won about $\frac{4}{9}$, $\frac{2}{3}$, and $\frac{5}{9}$ of their games. The denominator for Atlanta's record is not a 9. New York won more of its games than Philadelphia. About what fraction of its games did each team win?

Atlanta $\frac{6}{9}$

Philadelphia $\frac{4}{9}$

New York $\frac{5}{9}$

**16.** The three largest butterflies in the world are the Goliath, the Queen Alexandra, and the African swallowtail. Their wingspans are $9\frac{1}{10}$, $8\frac{3}{10}$, and 11 inches. The Queen Alexandra is the largest. The African swallowtail is larger than the Goliath. What are the wingspans of the three largest butterflies?

Goliath $8\frac{3}{10}$ in.

Queen Alexandra 11 in.

African swallowtail $9\frac{1}{10}$ in.

**Make a model to solve each problem.**

**17.** The track at the gym is $\frac{1}{3}$ mile long. The high school's track is $\frac{1}{12}$ mile longer than the gym's. How long is the high school track?

Answer ____________

**18.** Nando mixed $\frac{1}{4}$ gallon of red paint with $\frac{3}{8}$ gallon of white paint to make pink. How much pink paint did Nando mix?

Answer ____________

## Meaning of Decimals

Like fractions, **decimals** show parts of a whole. The shaded portion of each square can be written as a fraction or as a decimal.

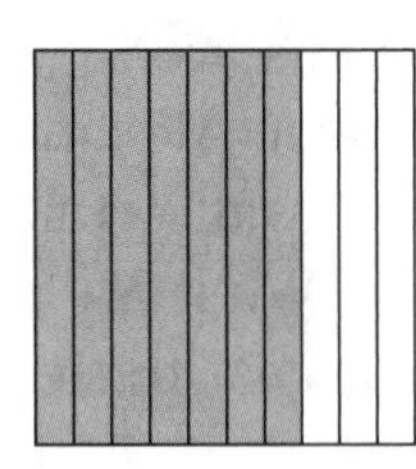

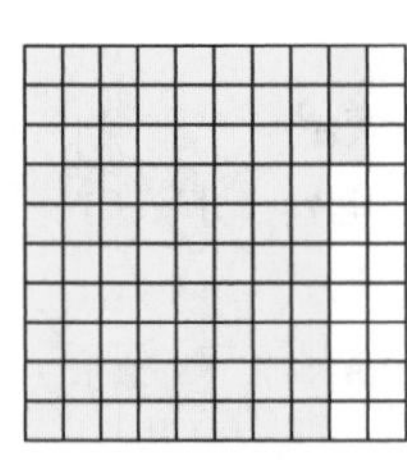

| | $\frac{1}{1}$ or 1 | $\frac{7}{10}$ or 0.7 | $\frac{83}{100}$ or 0.83 | $1\frac{5}{10}$ or 1.5 |
|---|---|---|---|---|
| **Read:** | **one** | **seven-tenths** | **eighty-three hundredths** | **one and five-tenths** |

**Remember,**

- **a *decimal point* separates a whole number and its decimal parts.**
- **a whole number has a decimal point, but it is usually not written. 2 is the same as 2.0.**
- **a decimal point is read as *and*.**

**Write the decimal shown by the shaded part of each figure.**

*a* *b* *c*

**1.**

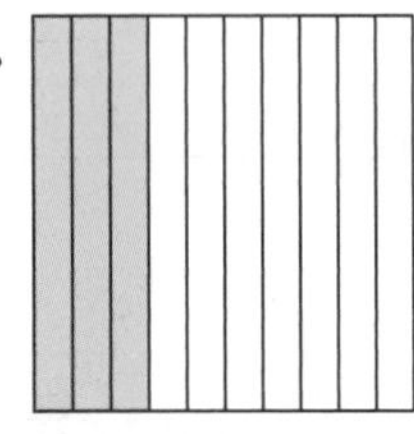

______

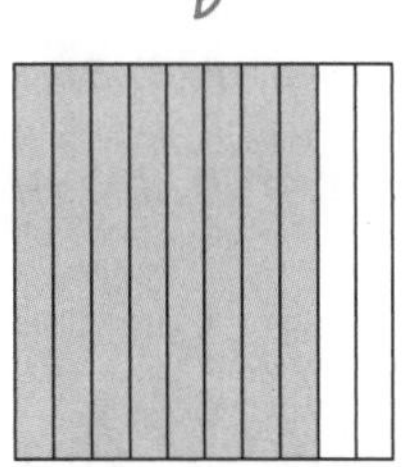

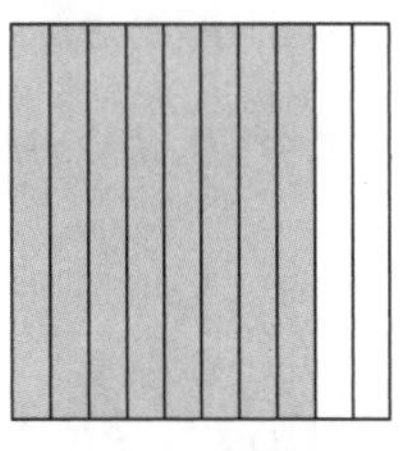

______

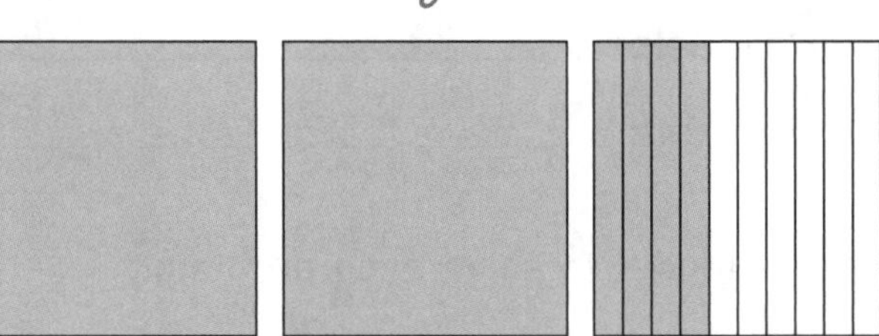

______

**2.**

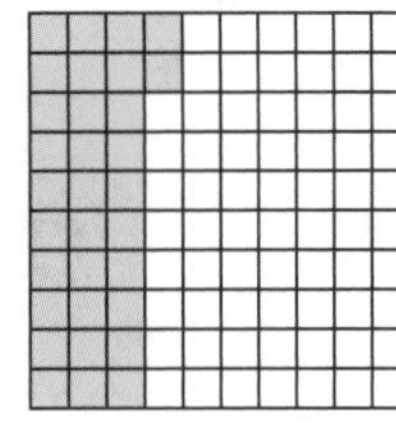

______

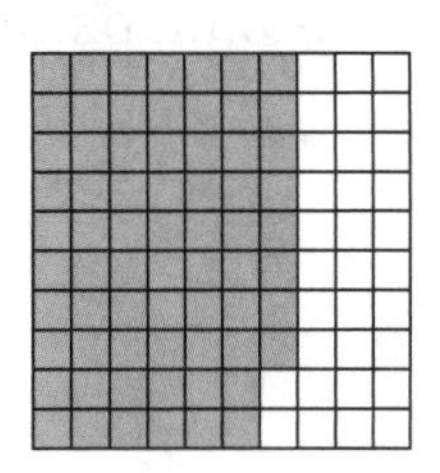

______

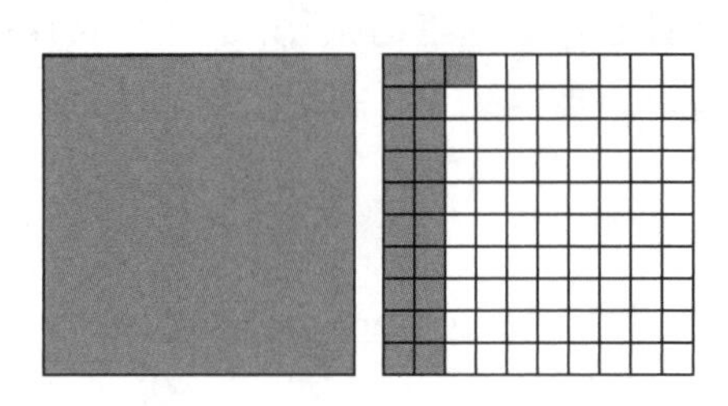

______

**Write each money amount with a dollar sign and a decimal point.**

*a* *b*

**3.** one dollar *$1.00* ten cents *$0.10*

**4.** twelve dollars ______ three dimes ______

# Decimal Place Value

You can use a place-value chart to help you understand decimal places.
The digits to the right of the decimal point show decimals.
The digits to the left of the decimal point show whole numbers.

The 2 is in the tens place.
Its value is 20 or 2 tens.

The **8** is in the ones place.
Its value is 8 or **8** ones.

The **6** is in the tenths place.
Its value is 0.6 or **6** tenths.

The **0** is in the hundredths place.
Its value is 0 or **0** hundredths.

The **3** is in the thousandths place.
Its value is 0.003 or **3** thousandths.

| hundreds | tens | ones | tenths | hundredths | thousandths |
|---|---|---|---|---|---|
| | 2 | 8. | 6 | 0 | 3 |

**whole numbers . decimals**

**Write each number in the place-value chart.**

1. 29.01
2. 0.485
3. 3.782
4. 67.567
5. 10.0
6. 142.04

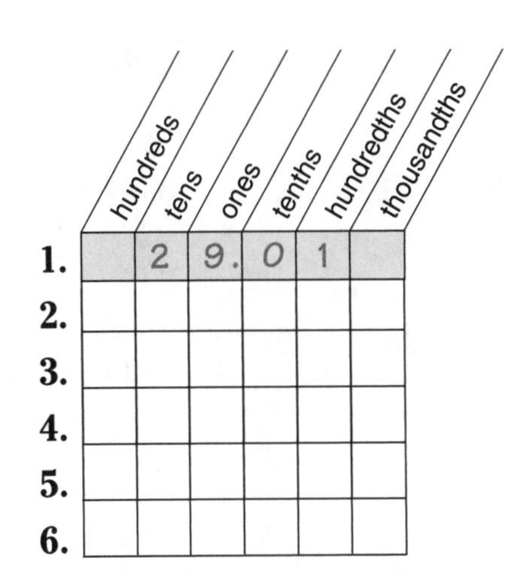


**Write the place name for the 7 in each number.**

| | a | b | c |
|---|---|---|---|
| **7.** | 2.73 *tenths* | 8.076 ______ | 12.687 ______ |
| **8.** | 0.017 ______ | 7.019 ______ | 6.007 ______ |
| **9.** | 10.47 ______ | 70.480 ______ | 0.760 ______ |

**Write the value of the underlined digit.**

| | a | b | c |
|---|---|---|---|
| **10.** | 0.223 *3 thousandths* | 0.194 ______ | 0.604 ______ |
| **11.** | 1.95 ______ | 3.008 ______ | 0.18 ______ |
| **12.** | 64.5 ______ | 4.678 ______ | 16.96 ______ |

# Reading and Writing Decimals

A place-value chart can help you understand how to read and write decimals.

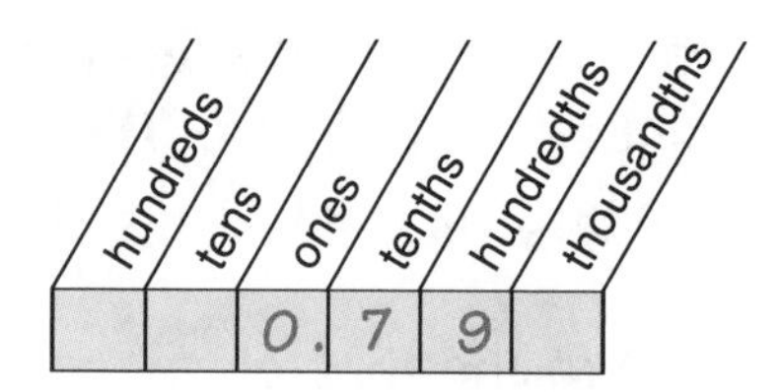


To read a decimal, read it as a whole number. Then name the place value of the last digit.

Read 0.79 as seventy-nine hundredths.

**To read a decimal that has a whole number part,**

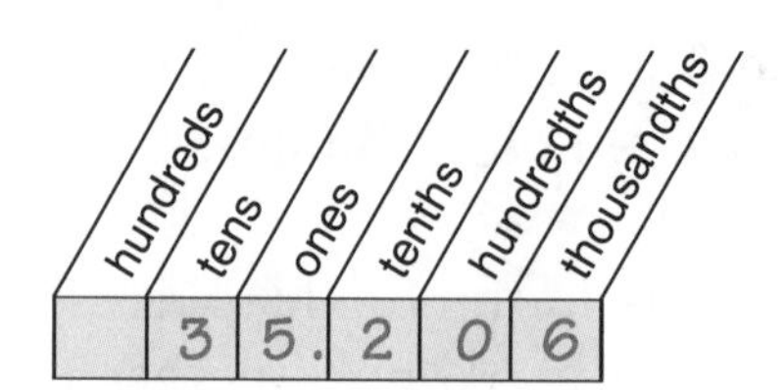


- **read the whole number part.**
- **read the decimal point as *and*.**
- **read the decimal part as a whole number and then name the place value of the last digit.**

Read 35.206 as thirty-five and two-hundred six thousandths.

**Write the place value of the last digit of the number.**

| | a | b | c |
|---|---|---|---|
| **1.** | 3.09 *hundredths* | 89.065 ________ | 0.4 ________ |
| **2.** | 12.1 ________ | 2.63 ________ | 4.002 ________ |
| **3.** | 0.4 ________ | 64.002 ________ | 640.20 ________ |

**Write as a decimal.**

| | a | b |
|---|---|---|
| **4.** | four tenths *0.4* | four hundredths ________ |
| **5.** | four thousandths ________ | five hundred four thousandths ________ |
| **6.** | sixteen thousandths ________ | sixteen hundredths ________ |
| **7.** | ten and thirteen hundredths ________ | fifty-four and one hundredth ________ |

**Write each decimal in words.**

**8.** 0.048 *forty-eight thousandths*

**9.** 0.64 ________________________

**10.** 9.4 ________________________

**Write as a decimal.**

| | *a* | *b* |
|---|---|---|
| **11.** | five tenths ______ | eighty-nine hundredths ______ |
| **12.** | three and four thousandths ______ | sixty-three hundredths ______ |
| **13.** | four and seven tenths ______ | eight and five hundredths ______ |
| **14.** | thirty-one hundredths ______ | twenty-eight thousandths ______ |
| **15.** | seventeen thousandths ______ | eight and nine thousandths ______ |
| **16.** | nine and nine hundredths ______ | twenty-three hundredths ______ |
| **17.** | seventy and one tenth ______ | seventy-one hundredths ______ |

**Write each decimal in words.**

**18.** 0.23 ______________________________

**19.** 0.8 ______________________________

**20.** 4.53 ______________________________

**21.** 6.009 ______________________________

**22.** 9.802 ______________________________

**23.** 18.04 ______________________________

**24.** 0.18 ______________________________

# Compare and Order Decimals

To compare two decimal numbers, begin at the left.

Compare the digits in each place value.

**The symbol $>$ means *is greater than.*** $1.9 > 1.2$
**The symbol $<$ means *is less than.*** $3.1 < 3.5$
**The symbol $=$ means *is equal to.*** $2.7 = 2.70$

**Compare: 1.5 and 1.4**

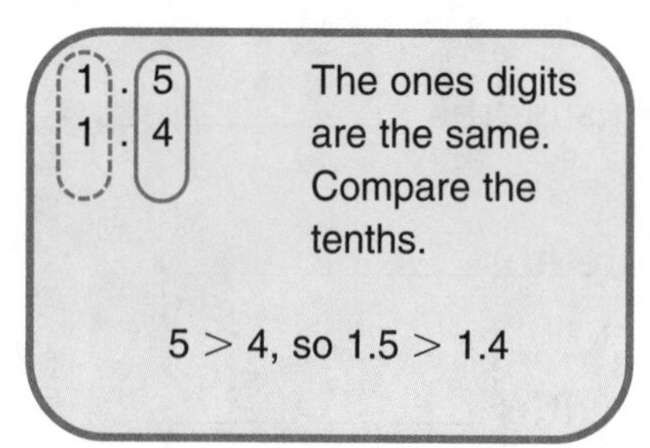

1 . 5
1 . 4
The ones digits are the same. Compare the tenths.
5 > 4, so 1.5 > 1.4


**Compare: $0.06 and $0.31**

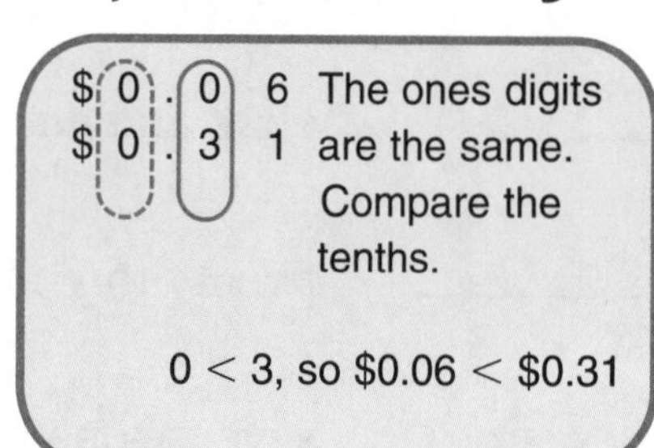

$ 0 . 0 6
$ 0 . 3 1
The ones digits are the same. Compare the tenths.
0 < 3, so $0.06 < $0.31


**Compare: 0.2 and 0.29**

0 . 2 0
0 . 2 9

Write a zero. The ones and tenths digits are the same. Compare the hundredths.

0 < 9, so 0.2 < 0.29

**Compare. Write <, >, or =.**

| | *a* | *b* | *c* |
|---|---|---|---|
| **1.** | 1.5 __<__ 1.9<br>1 . 5<br>1 . 9 | 1.3 ______ 1.8<br>1 . 3<br>1 . 8 | 3.5 ______ 3.3<br>3 . 5<br>3 . 3 |
| **2.** | $1.76 ______ $1.92 | $0.38 ______ $0.56 | $8.62 ______ $8.27 |
| **3.** | 0.49 ______ 0.490 | 0.890 ______ 0.089 | 0.134 ______ 0.143 |

**Write in order from least to greatest.**

| | *a* | *b* |
|---|---|---|
| **4.** | 14.0 1.4 140 __1.4 14.0 140__<br>14 . 0<br>1 . 4<br>140 | 0.7 0.007 0.07 ______ |
| **5.** | 345 3.45 34.5 ______ | 0.80 0.79 0.81 ______ |

**Compare. Write <, >, or =.**

| | *a* | *b* | *c* |
|---|---|---|---|
| **6.** | 6.210 ______ 6.201 | \$19.78 ______ \$19.87 | 58.9 ______ 59.0 |
| **7.** | 117.8 ______ 171.8 | 0.609 ______ 0.61 | 44.8 ______ 44.80 |
| **8.** | 6 ______ 6.0 | 27.9 ______ 2.79 | 15.34 ______ 5.434 |
| **9.** | 0.89 ______ 0.009 | 0.9 ______ 0.89 | \$0.09 ______ \$0.89 |
| **10.** | 61.4 ______ 61.40 | 6.315 ______ 6.31 | 200.0 ______ 200 |
| **11.** | 165 ______ 165.001 | 12.385 ______ 12.3 | 2.428 ______ 2.43 |

**Write in order from least to greatest.**

| | *a* | *b* |
|---|---|---|
| **12.** | \$17.0 \$1.70 \$170 ______________ | 0.06 0.60 0.066 ______________ |
| **13.** | 5.6 5.06 5.602 ______________ | 0.3 0.003 0.03 ______________ |
| **14.** | 1.2 21 2.1 ______________ | 0.090 0.8 0.007 ______________ |

2'5"
2'
1'5"
1"
"HE WAS LESS THAN SPOT OR SCRUFFY, BUT GREATER THAN FLUFFY OR PEPE."

# Fraction and Decimal Equivalents

Sometimes you will need to either change a decimal to a fraction or a fraction to a decimal.

To write a decimal as a fraction, identify the value of the last place in the decimal. Use this place value to write the denominator.

| Decimal | | Fraction or Mixed Number |
|---|---|---|
| 0.7 | = | $\frac{7}{10}$ |
| 0.59 | = | $\frac{59}{100}$ |
| 0.005 | = | $\frac{5}{1,000}$ |
| 3.47 | = | $3\frac{47}{100}$ or $\frac{347}{100}$ |

To write a fraction that has a denominator of 10, 100, or 1,000 as a decimal, write the digits from the numerator. Then write the decimal point.

| Fraction or Mixed Number | | Decimal |
|---|---|---|
| $\frac{3}{10}$ | = | 0.3 |
| $\frac{43}{100}$ | = | 0.43 |
| $\frac{529}{1,000}$ | = | 0.529 |
| $\frac{618}{100}$ or $6\frac{18}{100}$ | = | 6.18 |

**Write each decimal as a fraction.**

| | a | b | c | d |
|---|---|---|---|---|
| **1.** | 0.3 $\frac{3}{10}$ | 0.7 ______ | 0.9 ______ | 0.1 ______ |
| **2.** | 0.03 ______ | 0.07 ______ | 0.09 ______ | 0.01 ______ |

**Write each decimal as a mixed number.**

| | a | b | c | d |
|---|---|---|---|---|
| **3.** | 2.3 $2\frac{3}{10}$ | 6.9 ______ | 3.7 ______ | 8.1 ______ |
| **4.** | 9.88 ______ | 5.07 ______ | 4.90 ______ | 2.25 ______ |

**Write each fraction as a decimal.**

| | a | b | c | d |
|---|---|---|---|---|
| **5.** | $\frac{4}{10}$ 0.4 | $\frac{8}{10}$ ______ | $\frac{6}{10}$ ______ | $\frac{2}{10}$ ______ |
| **6.** | $\frac{23}{100}$ ______ | $\frac{97}{100}$ ______ | $\frac{246}{1,000}$ ______ | $\frac{810}{1,000}$ ______ |
| **7.** | $\frac{306}{100}$ ______ | $\frac{901}{100}$ ______ | $\frac{8,825}{1,000}$ ______ | $\frac{6,975}{1,000}$ ______ |

# Fraction and Decimal Equivalents

Not all fractions can be changed to decimal form easily. To write fractions that have denominators other than 10, 100, or 1,000 as decimals, first write an equivalent fraction that has a denominator of 10, 100, or 1,000. Then write the equivalent fraction as a decimal.

**Remember, not all fractions have simple decimal equivalents.**

**Examples:** $\frac{1}{3} = 0.333\ldots$ $\frac{1}{6} = 0.166\ldots$

**Write $\frac{1}{2}$ as a decimal.**

| Write $\frac{1}{2}$ with 10 as the denominator. | Write the fraction as a decimal. |
|---|---|
| $\frac{1}{2} = \frac{1 \times 5}{2 \times 5} = \frac{5}{10}$ | $= 0.5$ |

**Write $3\frac{1}{4}$ as a decimal.**

| Write $3\frac{1}{4}$ as an improper fraction. | Write the new fraction with 100 as the denominator. | Write the fraction as a decimal. |
|---|---|---|
| $3\frac{1}{4} = \frac{13}{4}$ | $\frac{13}{4} = \frac{13 \times 25}{4 \times 25} = \frac{325}{100}$ | $= 3.25$ |

**Write each fraction as a decimal.**

| | *a* | *b* | *c* |
|---|---|---|---|
| **1.** | $\frac{3}{4} = \frac{3 \times 25}{4 \times 25} = \frac{75}{100} = 0.75$ | $\frac{1}{5} =$ ______ | $\frac{24}{25} =$ ______ |
| **2.** | $\frac{4}{5} =$ ______ | $\frac{7}{20} =$ ______ | $\frac{3}{20} =$ ______ |
| **3.** | $\frac{6}{25} =$ ______ | $\frac{10}{20} =$ ______ | $\frac{13}{25} =$ ______ |
| **4.** | $\frac{17}{5} =$ ______ | $\frac{9}{2} =$ ______ | $\frac{51}{20} =$ ______ |
| **5.** | $\frac{68}{25} =$ ______ | $\frac{33}{4} =$ ______ | $\frac{34}{5} =$ ______ |

**Write each mixed number as a decimal.**

| | *a* | *b* |
|---|---|---|
| **6.** | $4\frac{3}{20} = \frac{83}{20} = \frac{83 \times 5}{20 \times 5} = \frac{415}{100} = 4.15$ | $20\frac{1}{5} =$ ______ |
| **7.** | $3\frac{2}{25} =$ ______ | $5\frac{22}{25} =$ ______ |

## Problem-Solving Method: Find a Pattern

Linda grew a plant for her science fair project. She measured and recorded the plant's height every week to track its growth. How fast did the plant grow?

| Week 1 | Week 2 | Week 3 | Week 4 | Week 5 |
|---|---|---|---|---|
| $1\frac{1}{10}$ inches | $1\frac{1}{5}$ inches | $1\frac{3}{10}$ inches | $1\frac{2}{5}$ inches | $1\frac{1}{2}$ inches |

**Understand the problem.**

- **What do you want to know?**
  how fast the plant grew

- **What information is given?**
  measurements for five weeks

**Plan how to solve it.**

- **What method can you use?**
  You can find a pattern.

**Solve it.**

- **How can you use this method to solve the problem?**
  Write each measurement as a decimal. Then look for a pattern between each week's height.

| | | | |
|---|---|---|---|
| **Week 1** | $1\frac{1}{10}$ inch | = | 1.1 |
| **Week 2** | $1\frac{1}{5}$ inch | = | 1.2 |
| **Week 3** | $1\frac{3}{10}$ inch | = | 1.3 |
| **Week 4** | $1\frac{2}{5}$ inch | = | 1.4 |
| **Week 5** | $1\frac{1}{2}$ inch | = | 1.5 |

← Each week the plant was 0.1 inch taller.

- **What is the answer?**
  The plant grew 0.1 inch, or $\frac{1}{10}$ inch, a week.

**Look back and check your answer.**

- **Is your answer reasonable?**
  You can check the pattern by adding $\frac{1}{10}$ inch to each week's height.

$1\frac{1}{10} + \frac{1}{10} = 1\frac{2}{10} = 1\frac{1}{5}$ inch

$1\frac{1}{5} + \frac{1}{10} = 1\frac{3}{10}$ inch

$1\frac{3}{10} + \frac{1}{10} = 1\frac{4}{10} = 1\frac{2}{5}$ inch

$1\frac{2}{5}$ inch $+ \frac{1}{10} = 1\frac{5}{10} = 1\frac{1}{2}$ inch

The sums match the growth pattern.
The answer is reasonable.

**Find a pattern to solve each problem.**

1. The African sharp-nosed frog is one of the best jumpers in the world. Complete the pattern below to find how far the frog would travel by the fourth jump.

| Jump 1 | Jump 2 | Jump 3 | Jump 4 |
|---|---|---|---|
| $4\frac{1}{2}$ in. | 9 in. | $13\frac{1}{2}$ in. | ? |

Answer ____________________

**Write the number pattern. Then answer the question.**

2. What is the next number in the pattern?

$\frac{9}{10}, \frac{4}{5}, \frac{7}{10}, \ldots$

Pattern ____________________

Answer ____________________

3. What is the next number in the pattern?

**8.72, 8.52, 8.32, . . .**

Pattern ____________________

Answer ____________________

4. A square can be made with 4 toothpicks. It takes 7 toothpicks to make two squares side by side. Three squares in a row can be made with 10 toothpicks. How many toothpicks would you need to make four squares in a row?

Pattern ____________________

Answer ____________________

5. The first five multiples of 11 are 11, 22, 33, 44, 55. Write the number pattern for the sum of the digits in each multiple. What would be the next number in this pattern?

Pattern ____________________

Answer ____________________

# Rounding Decimals

Rounding decimals can be used to tell **approximately** how many.
You can use a number line to round decimals.

**Remember, when a number is halfway, always round up.**

**Round 42.3 to the nearest one.**

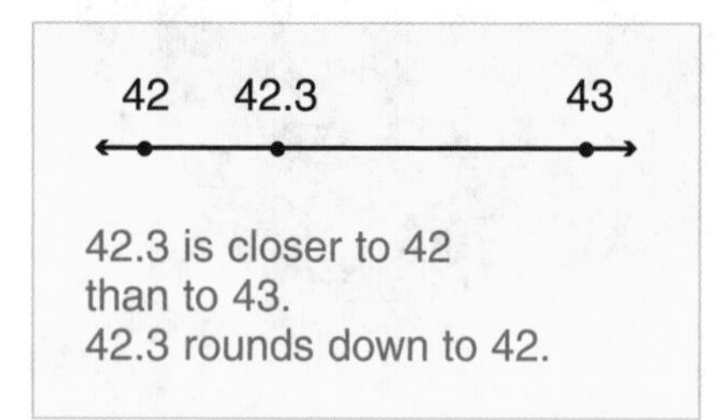

42
42.3
43
42.3 is closer to 42
than to 43.
42.3 rounds down to 42.


**Round $5.78 to the nearest dollar.**

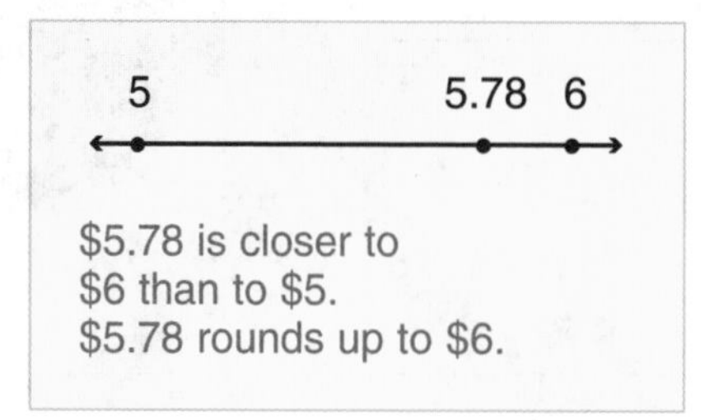

5
5.78
6
$5.78 is closer to
$6 than to $5.
$5.78 rounds up to $6.


**Round 7.25 to the nearest tenth.**

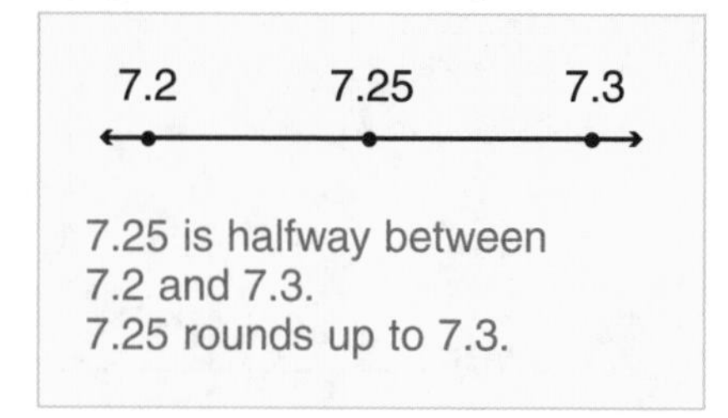

7.2
7.25
7.3
7.25 is halfway between
7.2 and 7.3.
7.25 rounds up to 7.3.


**Round to the nearest one.**

| | a | b | c | d |
|---|---|---|---|---|
| **1.** | 3.8 ___4___ | 2.5 ______ | 1.9 ______ | 7.3 ______ |
| **2.** | 39.6 ______ | 82.3 ______ | 78.9 ______ | 50.5 ______ |

**Round each amount to the nearest dollar.**

| | a | b | c | d |
|---|---|---|---|---|
| **3.** | $9.15 ___$9.00___ | $3.67 ______ | $1.42 ______ | $73.07 ______ |
| **4.** | $0.98 ______ | $3.49 ______ | $10.10 ______ | $25.50 ______ |

**Round to the nearest tenth.**

| | a | b | c | d |
|---|---|---|---|---|
| **5.** | 0.36 ___0.4___ | 0.72 ______ | 0.83 ______ | 0.45 ______ |
| **6.** | 82.78 ______ | 29.93 ______ | 85.54 ______ | 60.04 ______ |

# Addition of Decimals

To add decimals, line up the decimal points. Write zeros as needed. Then add as with whole numbers. Write a decimal point in the sum.

**Find: 5.7 + 6.84**

Write a zero.

| | T | O | Ts | Hs |
|---|---|---|---|---|
| | | 5 | .7 | 0 |
| + | | 6 | .8 | 4 |
| | | | | |

Add the hundredths.

| | T | O | Ts | Hs |
|---|---|---|---|---|
| | | 5 | .7 | 0 |
| + | | 6 | .8 | 4 |
| | | | | 4 |

Add the tenths. Regroup. Write a decimal point in the sum.

| | T | O | Ts | Hs |
|---|---|---|---|---|
| | | 1 | | |
| | | 5 | .7 | 0 |
| + | | 6 | .8 | 4 |
| | | | .5 | 4 |

Add the ones.

| | T | O | Ts | Hs |
|---|---|---|---|---|
| | | 1 | | |
| | | 5 | .7 | 0 |
| + | | 6 | .8 | 4 |
| | 1 | 2 | .5 | 4 |

**Add. Write zeros as needed.**

**1.**

*a*

| T | O | Ts |
|---|---|---|
| | 1 | |
| 1 | 2 | .7 |
| +1 | 3 | .8 |
| 2 | 6 | .5 |

*b*

| T | O | Ts |
|---|---|---|
| 4 | 9 | .5 |
| +2 | 7 | .3 |
| | | |

*c*

| T | O | Ts |
|---|---|---|
| 3 | 4 | .6 |
| +5 | 6 | .9 |
| | | |

*d*

| T | O | Ts |
|---|---|---|
| 6 | 2 | .7 |
| +1 | 4 | .5 |
| | | |

**2.**

*a*

| O | Ts | Hs | Ths |
|---|---|---|---|
| 1 | .2 | 4 | 5 |
| +7 | .5 | 6 | 8 |
| | | | |

*b*

| O | Ts | Hs | Ths |
|---|---|---|---|
| 3 | .5 | 1 | 8 |
| +2 | .3 | 6 | 4 |
| | | | |

*c*

| O | Ts | Hs | Ths |
|---|---|---|---|
| 7 | .0 | 0 | 5 |
| +2 | .9 | 8 | 6 |
| | | | |

*d*

| T | O | Ts | Hs | Ths |
|---|---|---|---|---|
| 1 | 6 | .1 | 3 | 6 |
| +4 | 8 | .0 | 5 | 4 |
| | | | | |

**3.**

*a*

| | T | O | Ts | Hs |
|---|---|---|---|---|
| | | 2 | .7 | 1 |
| | | 4 | .3 | 6 |
| + | | 3 | .0 | 8 |
| | | | | |

*b*

| O | Ts | Hs |
|---|---|---|
| 5 | .0 | 3 |
| 3 | .6 | 1 |
| +0 | .9 | 5 |
| | | |

*c*

| | T | O | Ts | Hs |
|---|---|---|---|---|
| | | 1 | .5 | |
| | | 7 | .3 | 9 |
| + | | 6 | .8 | |
| | | | | |

*d*

| | T | O | Ts | Hs |
|---|---|---|---|---|
| | | 6 | .4 | 7 |
| | | 2 | .8 | 9 |
| | | 3 | .1 | 5 |
| + | | 1 | .2 | 4 |
| | | | | |

**Add. Write zeros as needed.**

| | a | b | c |
|---|---|---|---|
| **1.** | 5.7<br>+0.2 | 4.4<br>+2.8 | 42.9<br>+33.5 |
| **2.** | 1.31<br>+6.02 | 2.32<br>+1.96 | 24.27<br>+13.64 |
| **3.** | \$32.51<br>+\$18.75 | \$6.32<br>+\$3.42 | \$57.94<br>+\$21.57 |
| **4.** | 165.3<br>+128.9 | 80.07<br>+18.6 | 0.89<br>+0.36 |

**Line up the digits. Then find the sums. Write zeros as needed.**

| | a | b | c |
|---|---|---|---|
| **5.** | 0.9 + 0.6 = ______<br>0.9<br>+0.6 | 1.7 + 2.8 = ______ | 54.3 + 41.5 = ______ |
| **6.** | \$6.37 + \$4.21 = ______ | \$0.23 + \$8.76 = ______ | \$67.95 + \$22.05 = ______ |
| **7.** | 8.815 + 0.173 = ______ | 4.321 + 9.876 = ______ | 2.843 + 1.562 = ______ |
| **8.** | 9.5 + 2 = ______ | 14 + 3.2 = ______ | 0.6 + 16 = ______ |

# Estimation of Decimal Sums

To estimate a decimal sum, first round the decimals to the same place value. Then add the rounded numbers.

**Estimate: $5.28 + $3.63**

Round each decimal to the nearest one. Add.

$5.28 → $5
+$3.63 → + 4
$9

**Estimate: 5.28 + 3.63**

Round each decimal to the nearest tenth. Add.

5.28 → 5.3
+3.63 → +3.6
8.9

**Estimate each sum by rounding to the nearest one.**

| | a | b | c | d |
|---|---|---|---|---|
| **1.** | 2.4 → 2<br>+6.8 → +7<br>9 | $5.02 →<br>+ 8.11 → | $72.6 →<br>+ 35.9 → | $48.35 →<br>+ 37.66 → |
| **2.** | 7.89 →<br>+8.9 → | 96.54 →<br>+22.18 → | 4.273 →<br>+3.79 → | 21.109 →<br>+18.381 → |

**Estimate each sum by rounding to the nearest tenth.**

| | a | b | c | d |
|---|---|---|---|---|
| **3.** | 0.93 → 0.9<br>+0.28 → +0.3<br>1.2 | 2.31 →<br>+4.53 → | 9.88 →<br>+7.43 → | $12.69 →<br>+ 86.76 → |
| **4.** | 38.52 →<br>+14.62 → | 0.385 →<br>+0.769 → | 3.269 →<br>+1.41 → | 5.73 →<br>+0.898 → |

# Subtraction of Decimals

To subtract decimals, line up the decimal points. Write zeros as needed.
Then subtract as with whole numbers. Write a decimal point in the difference.

**Find: 28.3 − 14.95**

Write a zero. Regroup. Subtract the hundredths.

| | T | O | Ts | Hs |
|---|---|---|---|---|
| | | | 2 | 10 |
| | 2 | 8 | .~~3~~ | ~~0~~ |
| − | 1 | 4 | .9 | 5 |
| | | | | 5 |

Regroup. Subtract the tenths. Write a decimal point in the difference.

| | T | O | Ts | Hs |
|---|---|---|---|---|
| | | | 12 | |
| | | 7 | ~~2~~ | 10 |
| | 2 | ~~8~~ | .~~3~~ | ~~0~~ |
| − | 1 | 4 | .9 | 5 |
| | | | .3 | 5 |

Subtract the ones.

| | T | O | Ts | Hs |
|---|---|---|---|---|
| | | | 12 | |
| | | 7 | ~~2~~ | 10 |
| | 2 | ~~8~~ | .~~3~~ | ~~0~~ |
| − | 1 | 4 | .9 | 5 |
| | | 3 | .3 | 5 |

Subtract the tens.

| | T | O | Ts | Hs |
|---|---|---|---|---|
| | | | 12 | |
| | | 7 | ~~2~~ | 10 |
| | 2 | ~~8~~ | .~~3~~ | ~~0~~ |
| − | 1 | 4 | .9 | 5 |
| | 1 | 3 | .3 | 5 |

**Subtract. Write zeros as needed.**

**1.**

*a*

| T | O | Ts |
|---|---|---|
| 5 | 12 | |
| ~~6~~ | ~~2~~ | .7 |
| −1 | 4 | .2 |
| 4 | 8 | .5 |

*b*

| T | O | Ts |
|---|---|---|
| 8 | 3 | .8 |
| −7 | 5 | .4 |
| | | |

*c*

| T | O | Ts | Hs |
|---|---|---|---|
| $5 | 3 | .8 | 2 |
| −$1 | 0 | .1 | 1 |
| | | | |

*d*

| T | O | Ts | Hs |
|---|---|---|---|
| $3 | 7 | .4 | 3 |
| −$2 | 9 | .5 | 2 |
| | | | |

**2.**

*a*

| O | Ts | Hs |
|---|---|---|
| 8 | .0 | 0 |
| −6 | .1 | 2 |
| | | |

*b*

| O | Ts | Hs |
|---|---|---|
| 8 | .6 | |
| −4 | .2 | 9 |
| | | |

*c*

| T | O | Ts | Hs |
|---|---|---|---|
| 2 | 3 | .5 | 4 |
| −1 | 2 | .6 | |
| | | | |

*d*

| T | O | Ts | Hs |
|---|---|---|---|
| 8 | 6 | .2 | 8 |
| −5 | 4 | | |
| | | | |

**3.**

*a*

| O | Ts | Hs | Ths |
|---|---|---|---|
| 9 | .2 | 1 | 0 |
| −0 | .8 | 4 | 7 |
| | | | |

*b*

| O | Ts | Hs | Ths |
|---|---|---|---|
| 7 | .5 | 1 | 6 |
| −5 | .2 | 8 | |
| | | | |

*c*

| O | Ts | Hs | Ths |
|---|---|---|---|
| 1 | .9 | | |
| −0 | .6 | 7 | 4 |
| | | | |

*d*

| T | O | Ts | Hs | Ths |
|---|---|---|---|---|
| 1 | 9 | .0 | 0 | 5 |
| −1 | 4 | .5 | | |
| | | | | |

**Subtract. Write zeros as needed.**

| | a | b | c | d |
|---|---|---|---|---|
| **4.** | $\begin{array}{r} 4.2 \\ -2.4 \\ \hline \end{array}$ | $\begin{array}{r} 16.5 \\ -13.9 \\ \hline \end{array}$ | $\begin{array}{r} 7.3 \\ -0.8 \\ \hline \end{array}$ | $\begin{array}{r} 9 \\ -5.6 \\ \hline \end{array}$ |
| **5.** | $\begin{array}{r} 5.45 \\ -0.16 \\ \hline \end{array}$ | $\begin{array}{r} 0.96 \\ -0.38 \\ \hline \end{array}$ | $\begin{array}{r} 22.77 \\ -11.88 \\ \hline \end{array}$ | $\begin{array}{l} 7.02 \\ -1.8 \\ \hline \end{array}$ |
| **6.** | $\begin{array}{r} \$6.28 \\ -\$2.64 \\ \hline \end{array}$ | $\begin{array}{r} \$3.42 \\ -\$0.78 \\ \hline \end{array}$ | $\begin{array}{r} \$17.63 \\ -\$13.45 \\ \hline \end{array}$ | $\begin{array}{r} \$30.00 \\ -\$19.25 \\ \hline \end{array}$ |

**Line up the digits. Then find the differences. Write zeros as needed.**

| | a | b | c |
|---|---|---|---|
| **7.** | $9.6 - 3.7 =$ ________ <br> $\begin{array}{r} 9.6 \\ -3.7 \\ \hline \end{array}$ | $7.02 - 1.86 =$ ________ | $4.007 - 2.628 =$ ________ |
| **8.** | $13.7 - 11.99 =$ ________ | $9.976 - 2.18 =$ ________ | $8.5 - 3.725 =$ ________ |

# Estimation of Decimal Differences

To estimate a decimal difference, first round the decimals to the same place value. Then subtract the rounded numbers.

**Estimate: $8.93 – $6.29**

Round each decimal to the nearest one.
Subtract.

| | | |
|---|---|---|
| $8.93 | → | $9 |
| − 6.29 | → | − 6 |
| | | $3 |

**Estimate: 8.93 – 6.29**

Round each decimal to the nearest tenth.
Subtract.

| | | |
|---|---|---|
| 8.93 | → | 8.9 |
| −6.29 | → | −6.3 |
| | | 2.6 |

**Estimate each difference by rounding to the nearest one.**

| | a | b | c | d |
|---|---|---|---|---|
| 1. | 6.1 → 6<br>−2.8 → −3<br>3 | $9.07 →<br>−$5.35 → | 15.9 →<br>−11.2 → | $42.57 →<br>−$27.83 → |
| 2. | 7.4 →<br>−6.34 → | 3.944 →<br>−1.351 → | 16.17 →<br>−10.682 → | 38.9 →<br>−13.667 → |

**Estimate each difference by rounding to the nearest tenth.**

| | a | b | c | d |
|---|---|---|---|---|
| 3. | 0.82 → 0.8<br>−0.39 → −0.4<br>0.4 | 4.64 →<br>−2.13 → | 25.27 →<br>−16.51 → | 32.08 →<br>−19.75 → |
| 4. | 47.023 →<br>−39.345 → | 5.37 →<br>−4.6 → | 63.87 →<br>−10.154 → | 9.2 →<br>−7.595 → |

## Problem-Solving Method: Use Estimation

Evan has $100.00 to buy art supplies. He wants to buy an easel for $46.75, a canvas for $31.99, and a new brush for $11.50. Does he have enough money to buy all the supplies?

**Understand the problem.**

- **What do you want to know?**
  if Evan has enough money for the art supplies

- **What information is given?**
  He has $100.00.
  The easel is $46.75, the canvas is $31.99, and the brush is $11.50.

**Plan how to solve it.**

- **What method can you use?**
  Since the problem is not asking for an exact answer, you can use estimation to find the sum of the art supply prices.

**Solve it.**

- **How can you use this method to solve the problem?**
  Round the prices to the nearest whole dollar. Then add.

$$\begin{array}{rcr} \$46.75 & \rightarrow & \$47 \\ 31.99 & \rightarrow & 32 \\ +\ 11.50 & \rightarrow & +\ 12 \\ \hline & & \$91 \end{array}$$

- **What is the answer?**
  Yes, $100.00 is enough to buy all the art supplies.

**Look back and check your answer.**

- **Is your answer reasonable?**
  You can check your estimate by finding the exact answer.

$$\begin{array}{r} \$46.75 \\ 31.99 \\ +\ 11.50 \\ \hline \$90.24 \end{array}$$

The exact answer is less than $100.00 and close to the estimate. The estimate is reasonable.

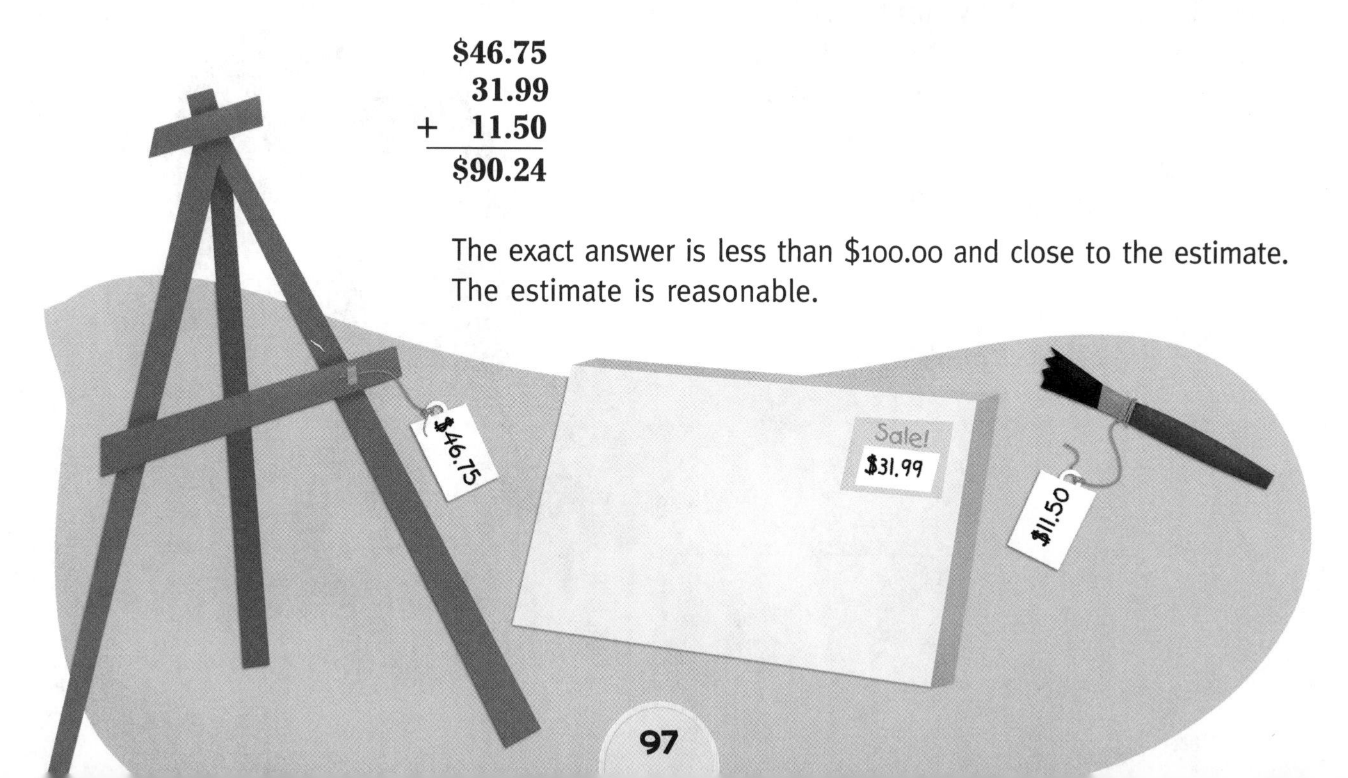

**Use estimation to solve each problem.**

1. Tyler bought a tennis racket for $54.99, a can of tennis balls for $8.53, and a new hat for $7.63. About how much did he spend in all at the sporting goods store that day?

Answer ________________

2. The average blue whale is 33.5 meters long. The average pilot whale is 6.4 meters long. About how much longer is a blue whale than a pilot whale?

Answer ________________

3. Blue Canyon, California, gets about 240.8 inches of snow every year. Marquette, Michigan, gets 129.2 inches and Sault Ste. Marie, Michigan, gets 116.1 inches each year. It snows in these three cities more than anywhere else in the United States. About how much snow do they get each year altogether?

Answer ________________

4. The world's largest ice cream sundae was made in 1988. It used 18.38 tons of ice cream and 4.25 tons of syrup and toppings. About how many whole tons did the sundae weigh altogether?

Answer ________________

5. It takes Jupiter 11.9 years to orbit, or go around, the sun. Saturn takes 17.6 more years than Jupiter to orbit the sun. About how long does it take Saturn to orbit the sun?

Answer ________________

# UNIT 5 Review

**Write the place name for the 8 in each number.**

| | a | b | c |
|---|---|---|---|
| **1.** | 0.583 ________ | 6.038 ________ | 7.82 ________ |

**Write the value of the underlined digit.**

| | a | b | c |
|---|---|---|---|
| **2.** | $0.\underline{3}14$ ________ | $0.6\underline{0}2$ ________ | $0.07\underline{9}$ ________ |

**Write as a decimal.**

| | a | b |
|---|---|---|
| **3.** | fourteen thousandths ________ | seven hundredths ________ |

**Write each decimal in words.**

**4.** 8.52 ____________________

**5.** 12.023 ____________________

**Compare. Write <, >, or =.**

| | a | b | c |
|---|---|---|---|
| **6.** | 0.3 ____ 0.6 | 2.95 ____ 2.59 | 0.246 ____ 0.426 |

**Write in order from least to greatest.**

| | a | b |
|---|---|---|
| **7.** | 0.53 0.32 0.42 ________ | 0.33 0.033 0.303 ________ |

**Write each fraction as a decimal.**

| | a | b | c | d |
|---|---|---|---|---|
| **8.** | $\frac{7}{10}$ ________ | $\frac{82}{100}$ ________ | $\frac{2}{5}$ ________ | $\frac{29}{2}$ ________ |

**Write each mixed number as a decimal.**

| | a | b | c |
|---|---|---|---|
| **9.** | $2\frac{7}{10}$ ________ | $12\frac{4}{5}$ ________ | $8\frac{7}{20}$ ________ |

# UNIT 5 Review

**Write each decimal as a fraction or mixed number.**

| | a | b | c | d |
|---|---|---|---|---|
| **10.** | 0.41 ______ | 0.063 ______ | 0.8 ______ | 3.17 ______ |

**Round to the nearest tenth.**

| | a | b | c | d |
|---|---|---|---|---|
| **11.** | 0.43 ______ | 0.75 ______ | 0.86 ______ | 0.98 ______ |

**Round to the nearest one.**

| | a | b | c | d |
|---|---|---|---|---|
| **12.** | 14.6 ______ | 6.5 ______ | 19.8 ______ | \$13.44 ______ |

**Add or subtract. Write zeros as needed.**

| | a | b | c | d | e |
|---|---|---|---|---|---|
| **13.** | 7.2 + 5.3 | 6.47 + 1.09 | 75.344 + 12.951 | 3.2 + 7.4 + 2.6 | 5.32 + 1.97 + 1.72 |
| **14.** | 6.3 − 4.7 | 3.712 − 2.123 | 16.80 − 7.17 | 9.053 − 8.443 | 7.136 − 4.901 |

**Estimate by rounding to the nearest one.**

| | a | b | c | d |
|---|---|---|---|---|
| **15.** | 8.6 → <br> +4.3 → | \$7.65 → <br> − 3.14 → | 69.75 → <br> +24.31 → | 11.20 → <br> − 4.19 → |

**Estimate by rounding to the nearest tenth.**

| | a | b | c | d |
|---|---|---|---|---|
| **16.** | 3.75 → <br> −2.17 → | 39.33 → <br> − 6.88 → | 2.323 → <br> +1.010 → | 16.49 → <br> + 23.41 → |

**Find a pattern to solve each problem.**

**17.** Kurt measured and recorded the corn plant's height every week to track its growth. How fast did the corn grow?

| Week 1 | Week 2 | Week 3 | Week 4 |
|---|---|---|---|
| 6 in. | $7\frac{1}{4}$ in. | $8\frac{1}{2}$ in. | $9\frac{3}{4}$ in. |

Answer ____________________

**18.** Maggie kept a running journal for four months. She wrote down her total miles for each month. By how many miles did she increase her work-outs each month?

| Jan. | Feb. | March | April |
|---|---|---|---|
| 31.4 | 35.6 | 39.8 | 44 |

Answer ____________________

**Use estimation to solve each problem.**

**19.** In 1900 in the United States, the life expectancy for women was 48.7 years. In 1999, the life expectancy for women was 76.1 years. About how much longer could a woman in the U.S. expect to live in 1999 than in 1900?

Answer ____________________

**20.** A black vulture has a wingspan 3.1 meters wide. A great bustard is the heaviest bird that can fly. Its wingspan is 2.7 meters. About how many meters wider is a black vulture's wingspan than a great bustard's?

Answer ____________________

**21.** It takes Neptune 164.8 years to orbit the sun. Pluto takes 82.9 more years than Neptune to orbit the sun. About how long does it take Pluto to orbit the sun?

Answer ____________________

# Unit 6
## Measurement

### Customary Length

The customary units that are used to measure length are **inch, foot, yard,** and **mile**.
The chart gives the relationship of one unit to another.

- A business envelope is about 10 inches long.
- A basketball hoop is about 10 feet high.

**1 foot (ft.) = 12 inches (in.)**
**1 yard (yd.) = 3 ft.**
**= 36 in.**
**1 mile (mi.) = 1,760 yd.**
**= 5,280 ft.**

You can multiply or divide to change units of measurement.

**Find: 5 yd. = ________ ft.**

To change larger units to smaller units, multiply.

1 yd. = 3 ft.

$5 \times 3 = 15$

5 yd. = 15 ft.

**Find: 18 in. = ________ ft.**

To change smaller units to larger units, divide.

12 in. = 1 ft.

$18 \div 12 = 1\frac{6}{12}$ or $1\frac{1}{2}$

18 in. = $1\frac{1}{2}$ ft.

**Choose the most appropriate unit of measure. Write *in., ft.,* or *mi.***

| | a | b |
|---|---|---|
| **1.** | length of a new pencil in. | height of a telephone pole ________ |

**Use the chart to complete the following.**

| | a | b |
|---|---|---|
| **2.** | 36 in. = 1 yd. | 12 in. = ________ ft. |
| **3.** | 1,760 yd. = ________ mi. | 1 yd. = ________ in. |

**Change each measurement to the smaller unit.**

| | a | b |
|---|---|---|
| **4.** | 7 ft. = 84 in. | 15 yd. = ________ ft. |
| **5.** | 6 yd. = ________ in. | 2 mi. = ________ ft. |

**Change each measurement to the larger unit.**

| | a | b |
|---|---|---|
| **6.** | 42 in. = $3\frac{1}{2}$ ft. | 72 in. = ________ yd. |
| **7.** | 35 in. = ________ ft. | 17 ft. = ________ yd. |

# Customary Weight

The customary units that are used to measure weight are **ounce, pound,** and **ton**.
The chart shows the relationship of one unit to another.

| **1 pound (lb.) = 16 ounces (oz.)** |
|---|
| **1 ton (T.) = 2,000 pounds** |

- A stick of margarine weighs 4 ounces.
- A small loaf of bread weighs about 1 pound.
- An elephant weighs about 7 tons.

**Find: 3 lb. = ________ oz.**

To change larger units to smaller units, multiply.

1 lb. = 16 oz.

$3 \times 16 = 48$

3 lb.= 48 oz.

**Find: 5,000 lb. = ________ T.**

To change smaller units to larger units, divide.

2,000 lb. = 1 T.

$5{,}000 \div 2{,}000 = 2\frac{1}{2}$

5,000 lb. = $2\frac{1}{2}$ T.

**Choose the most appropriate unit of measure. Write *oz., lb.,* or *T.***

| | a | b |
|---|---|---|
| **1.** | weight of a cat ___lb.___ | weight of a pick-up truck ________ |
| **2.** | weight of a tennis ball ________ | weight of a tiger ________ |

**Use the chart to complete the following.**

| | a | b | c |
|---|---|---|---|
| **3.** | 16 oz. = ___1___ lb. | 2,000 lb. = ________ T. | 1 lb. = ________ oz. |

**Change each measurement to the smaller unit.**

| | a | b | c |
|---|---|---|---|
| **4.** | 5 lb. = ___80___ oz. | 2 T. = ________ lb. | 2 lb. = ________ oz. |

**Change each measurement to the larger unit.**

| | a | b | c |
|---|---|---|---|
| **5.** | 24 oz. = ___$1\frac{1}{2}$___ lb. | 6,000 lb. = ________ T. | 3,000 lb. = ________ T. |
| **6.** | 36 oz. = ________ lb. | 92 oz. = ________ lb. | 50 oz. = ________ lb. |

# Customary Capacity

The customary units that are used to measure capacity are **cup, pint, quart,** and **gallon.** The chart shows the relationship of one unit to another.

- A drinking glass holds 1 cup of liquid.
- A small pan for cooking holds 1 quart.
- A large water pitcher holds 1 gallon.

| | |
|---|---|
| **1 pint (pt.)** | **= 2 cups (c.)** |
| **1 quart (qt.)** | **= 2 pt.** |
| | **= 4 c.** |
| **1 gallon (gal.)** | **= 4 qt.** |
| | **= 8 pt.** |
| | **= 16 c.** |

**Find: 7 qt. = ________ pt.**

To change larger units to smaller units, multiply.

1 qt. = 2 pt.

$7 \times 2 = 14$

7 qt. = 14 pt.

**Find: 10 pt. = ________ gal.**

To change smaller units to larger units, divide.

8 pt. = 1 gal.

$10 \div 8 = 1\frac{2}{8}$ or $1\frac{1}{4}$

10 pt. = $1\frac{1}{4}$ gal.

**Choose the most appropriate unit of measure. Write *c., pt., qt.,* or *gal.***

| | *a* | *b* |
|---|---|---|
| **1.** | capacity of a cereal bowl ________ | capacity of a fish tank ________ |

**Use the chart to complete the following.**

| | *a* | *b* | *c* |
|---|---|---|---|
| **2.** | 2 c. = ________ pt. | 2 pt. = ________ qt. | 4 qt. = ________ gal. |

**Change each measurement to the smaller unit.**

| | *a* | *b* | *c* |
|---|---|---|---|
| **3.** | 7 qt. = ________ c. | 3 gal. = ________ c. | 8 pt. = ________ c. |
| **4.** | 16 pt. = ________ c | 25 qt. = ________ c. | 50 gal. = ________ c. |

**Change each measurement to the larger unit.**

| | *a* | *b* | *c* |
|---|---|---|---|
| **5.** | 24 c. = ________ gal. | 12 c. = ________ qt. | 8 pt. = ________ gal. |
| **6.** | 10 c. = ________ qt. | 15 pt. = ________ gal. | 28 c. = ________ gal. |

# Comparing Customary Units

To compare two measurements, first change them to the same unit.

**Remember, to change larger units to smaller units, multiply.**

**Compare: 2 ft. to 30 in.**

**Think:** 1 ft. = 12 in.
2 ft. = $2 \times 12 = 24$ in.

24 in. ___*is less than*___ 30 in.

2 ft. ___$<$___ 30 in.

**Compare: 20 qt. to 4 gal.**

**Think:** 1 gal. = 4 qt.
4 gal. = $4 \times 4 = 16$ qt.

20 qt. ___*is greater than*___ 16 qt.

20 qt. ___$>$___ 4 gal.

**Compare. Write $<$, $>$, or $=$.**

| | *a* | *b* |
|---|---|---|
| **1.** | 48 oz. ___=___ 3 lb.<br>*1 lb. = 16 oz.*<br>*3 lb. = 3 × 16 = 48 oz.* | 36 c. ________ 2 qt. |
| **2.** | 3 mi. ________ 2,000 yd. | 3 T. ________ 6,000 lb. |
| **3.** | 24 ft. ________ 6 yd. | 6 pt. ________ 10 c. |
| **4.** | 2 mi. ________ 5,280 ft. | 6 lb. ________ 100 oz. |
| **5.** | 10 yd. ________ 40 ft. | 5 T. ________ 9,000 lb. |
| **6.** | 40 qt. ________ 6 gal. | 12 ft. ________ 144 in. |

# Metric Length: Meter and Kilometer

The **meter** (m) is the basic metric unit of length.
A baseball bat is about 1 meter long.

A **kilometer** (km) is one thousand meters.
(**Kilo** means 1,000.)
The kilometer is used to measure long distances.
The distance from New York City to Chicago is 1,140 km.

**1 km = 1,000 m**
**1 m = 0.001 km**

**Find: 8 km = ________ m**

To change larger units to smaller units, multiply.

1 km = 1,000 m

$8 \times 1{,}000 = 8{,}000$

8 km = 8,000 m

**Find: 6,000 m = ________ km**

To change smaller units to larger units, divide.

1,000 m = 1 km

$6{,}000 \div 1{,}000 = 6$

6,000 m = 6 km

**Choose the most appropriate unit of measure. Write *m* or *km*.**

| | *a* | *b* |
|---|---|---|
| **1.** | distance between cities ________ | height of a jogger ________ |
| **2.** | length of a city block ________ | distance to the moon ________ |

**Circle the best measurement.**

| | *a* | *b* |
|---|---|---|
| **3.** | distance between airports<br>125 m 125 km | height of a ceiling<br>2.8 m 2.8 km |
| **4.** | length of six automobiles<br>30 m 30 km | distance walked in one hour<br>6 m 5 km |

**Change each measurement to the smaller unit.**

| | *a* | *b* | *c* |
|---|---|---|---|
| **5.** | 7 km = 7,000 m | 3 km = ________ m | 57 km = ________ m |

**Change each measurement to the larger unit.**

| | *a* | *b* | *c* |
|---|---|---|---|
| **6.** | 2,000 m = 2 km | 6,000 m = ________ km | 10,000 m = ________ km |

# Metric Length: Centimeter and Millimeter

A meter (m) can be measured with a **meter stick**.

1 cm

1 mm

A **centimeter** (cm) is one hundredth of a meter. (**Centi** means 0.01.) The centimeter is used to measure small lengths. The length of a pencil is about 18 cm.

A **millimeter** (mm) is one thousandth of a meter. (**Milli** means 0.001.) The millimeter is used to measure very small lengths. The width of a housefly is about 5 mm.

**1 m = 100 cm**
**= 1,000 mm**
**1 cm = 0.01 m**
**= 10 mm**
**1 mm = 0.1 cm**
**= 0.001 m**

**Choose the most appropriate unit of measure. Write *m, cm,* or *mm*.**

| | *a* | *b* |
|---|---|---|
| **1.** | width of your book ________ | length of a safety pin ________ |
| **2.** | height of a honeybee ________ | length of your shoe ________ |
| **3.** | length of a basketball court ________ | thickness of a penny ________ |

**Circle the best measurement.**

| | *a* | *b* |
|---|---|---|
| **4.** | width of your fingernail<br>1 cm 1 m | length of a football field<br>100 m 100 cm |
| **5.** | width of a couch<br>3 m 3 mm | length of a notebook<br>25 cm 25 m |

**Change each measurement to the smaller unit.**

| | *a* | *b* |
|---|---|---|
| **6.** | 5 cm = ________ mm | 12 m = ________ cm |

**Change each measurement to the larger unit.**

| | *a* | *b* |
|---|---|---|
| **7.** | 20 mm = ________ cm | 500 cm = ________ m |

# Metric Mass

| 1 kg = 1,000 g |
|---|
| 1 g = 0.001 kg |

The **mass** of an object is not often measured outside the field of science. Mass measures the amount of matter in an object.

The **gram** (g) is the basic unit of mass. The gram is used to measure the mass of very light objects. A paper clip equals about 1 gram.

The **kilogram** (kg) is one thousand grams. It is used to measure the mass of heavier objects. A baseball bat equals about 1 kg. Remember, **kilo** means 1,000.

**Find: 5 kg = ________ g**

To change larger units to smaller units, multiply.

1 kg = 1,000 g

*5 × 1,000 = 5,000*

*5 kg = 5,000 g*

**Find: 4,000 g = ________ kg**

To change smaller units to larger units, divide.

1,000 g = 1 kg

*4,000 ÷ 1,000 = 4*

*4,000 g = 4 kg*

**Choose the most appropriate unit of measure. Write *g* or *kg*.**

| | *a* | *b* |
|---|---|---|
| **1.** | mass of a textbook ________ | mass of a nickel ________ |
| **2.** | mass of a football ________ | mass of a television ________ |

**Circle the best measurement.**

| | *a* | *b* |
|---|---|---|
| **3.** | mass of a dog<br>9 g 9 kg | mass of a spoonful of salt<br>1 kg 1 g |
| **4.** | mass of a loaf of bread<br>500 g 500 kg | mass of a bicycle<br>18 g 18 kg |

**Change each measurement to the smaller unit.**

| | *a* | *b* | *c* |
|---|---|---|---|
| **5.** | 9 kg = *9,000* g | 7 kg = ________ g | 13 kg = ________ g |

**Change each measurement to the larger unit.**

| | *a* | *b* | *c* |
|---|---|---|---|
| **6.** | 4,000 g = *4* kg | 2,000 g = ________ kg | 15,000 g = ________ kg |

# Metric Capacity

| 1 L = 1,000 mL |
|---|
| 1 mL = 0.001 L |

The **liter** (L) is the basic metric unit of capacity.
A liter of liquid will fill a box 10 centimeters on each side.
A large bottle of soda holds about 2 liters.

A **milliliter** (mL) is one thousandth of a liter.
It is used to measure very small amounts of liquid. A milliliter of liquid will fill a box 1 centimeter on each side. An eyedropper holds about 2 mL.

**Remember, *milli* means 0.001.**

**Choose the most appropriate unit of measure. Write *L* or *mL*.**

| | a | b |
|---|---|---|
| 1. | capacity of a tablespoon ________ | capacity of a water jug ________ |
| 2. | capacity of a bathtub ________ | capacity of a test tube ________ |

**Circle the best measurement.**

| | a | b |
|---|---|---|
| 3. | capacity of a swimming pool<br>5,000 mL 5,000 L | capacity of a jug of apple cider<br>4 mL 4 L |
| 4. | capacity of a teapot<br>700 mL 700 L | capacity of a bowl<br>180 mL 180 L |

**Change each measurement to the smaller unit.**

| | a | b | c |
|---|---|---|---|
| 5. | 10 L = 10,000 mL | 4 L = ________ mL | 250 L = ________ mL |

**Change each measurement to the larger unit.**

| | a | b | c |
|---|---|---|---|
| 6. | 5,000 mL = 5 L | 6,000 mL = ________ L | 30,000 mL = ________ L |

# Relating Units

The basic metric units are meter (m), liter (L), and gram (g). They are used with **prefixes** to form larger and smaller units.

Examples:

- **Kilo-** plus **gram** is kilogram (kg).
  Since kg means 1,000 g, kg is larger than g.
- **Centi-** plus **meter** is centimeter (cm).
  Since cm mean 0.01 m, cm is smaller than m.
- **Milli-** plus **liter** is milliliter (mL).
  Since mL means 0.001 L, mL is smaller than L.

larger ↑ / smaller ↓

| Prefix | Symbol | Meaning |
| --- | --- | --- |
| kilo- | k | 1,000 |
| base unit | m, L, g | 1 |
| centi- | c | 0.01 |
| milli- | m | 0.001 |

**Decide whether the following units are larger or smaller than the base unit. Then write < or >.**

| | a | b | c |
| --- | --- | --- | --- |
| **1.** | kL __>__ L | km _____ m | cg _____ g |
| **2.** | cm _____ m | cL _____ L | mg _____ g |
| **3.** | kg _____ g | mm _____ m | mL _____ L |

**Give the value of each unit. Use the values in the table.**

| | a | b | c |
| --- | --- | --- | --- |
| **4.** | kL = __1,000__ L | cg = _____ g | cL = _____ L |
| **5.** | cm = _____ m | mm = _____ m | mg = _____ g |

**Decide which is larger or smaller. Then write < or >.**

| | a | b | c |
| --- | --- | --- | --- |
| **6.** | kL __>__ mL | mL _____ cL | cg _____ kg |
| **7.** | mg _____ cg | km _____ cm | cm _____ mm |

# Comparing Metric Units

To compare two measurements, first change them to the same unit.

**Remember, to change larger units to smaller units, multiply.**

**Compare: 3 m to 400 cm**

**Think:** 1 m = 100 cm
3 m = 3 × 100 = 300 cm

300 cm *is less than* 400 cm

3 m < 400 cm

**Compare: 7,500 mL to 6 L**

**Think:** 1 L = 1,000 mL
6 L = 6 × 1,000 = 6,000 mL

7,500 mL *is greater than* 6,000 mL

7,500 mL > 6 L

**Compare. Write <, >, or =.**

| | *a* | *b* |
|---|---|---|
| **1.** | 3 kg ___=___ 3,000 g<br>*1 kg = 1,000 g*<br>*3 kg = 3 × 1,000 = 3,000 g* | 5 km ______ 4,500 m |
| **2.** | 32 cm ______ 300 mm | 62 L ______ 6,000 mL |
| **3.** | 5 m ______ 5,000 mm | 25 km ______ 25,000 m |
| **4.** | 600 cm ______ 6 m | 29,456 g ______ 2 kg |
| **5.** | 5,500 mL ______ 5 L | 54 m ______ 54,000 cm |
| **6.** | 40 kg ______ 685 g | 250 cm ______ 25,000 mm |

## Problem-Solving Method: Guess and Check

Every day, a vampire bat drinks half of its own body weight in blood. A mosquito can drink about $\frac{1}{10}$ the amount of blood a vampire bat drinks. Together, the mosquito and bat drink 33 milliliters of blood. How much blood does a vampire bat drink every day?

**Understand the problem.**

- **What do you want to know?**
  how much blood a vampire bat drinks each day

- **What information is given?**
  **Clue 1:** $\frac{1}{10}$ of bat's meal = mosquito's meal
  **Clue 2:** bat's meal + mosquito's meal = 33 mL

**Plan how to solve it.**

- **What method can you use?**
  You can guess an answer that satisfies one clue.
  Then check to see if your answer satisfies the other clue.

**Solve it.**

- **How can you use this method to solve the problem?**
  Try to guess in an organized way so that each of your guesses gets closer to the exact answer. Use a table.
  (Remember, to find $\frac{1}{2}$ of 8, divide 8 by 2. $\frac{1}{2}$ of 8 = 8 ÷ 2 = 4)

| Guess Bat Drink | Check Clue 1 | Check Clue 2 | Evaluate the Guess |
|---|---|---|---|
| 10 mL | $\frac{1}{10}$ of 10 = 1 | 10 + 1 = 11 | too low |
| 50 mL | $\frac{1}{10}$ of 50 = 5 | 50 + 5 = 55 | too high |
| 40 mL | $\frac{1}{10}$ of 40 = 4 | 40 + 4 = 44 | too high |
| 30 mL | $\frac{1}{10}$ of 30 = 3 | 30 + 3 = 33 | satisfies both clues |

- **What is the answer?**
  A vampire bat drinks 30 mL of blood every day.

**Look back and check your answer.**

- **Is your answer reasonable?**
  You can check division with multiplication and addition with subtraction.

  **10 × 3 = 30**
  **33 − 3 = 30**

  The amount satisfies both clues.
  The answer is reasonable.

**Use guess and check to solve each problem.**

1. Kendra is twice as old as Tim. In 10 years, Kendra will be four years older than Tim. How old are Kendra and Tim now?

Answer ______________________

2. Rita has five United States coins. Their total value is 31 cents. What coins and how many of each does she have?

Answer ______________________

3. A gray whale usually weighs 3 times as much as a baird's whale. The sum of their weights is 48 tons. How much does each whale usually weigh?

Answer ______________________

4. Vatican City and Monaco are the two smallest countries. Together, they only cover about 2.3 square kilometers. Monaco is 1.3 square km bigger than Vatican City. How big is each country?

Answer ______________________

5. A hot dog has about $\frac{1}{4}$ the amount of protein as 3 ounces of hamburger. Together, they have about 25 grams of protein. How many grams of protein are in a 3-oz. hamburger?

Answer ______________________

# UNIT 6 Review

**Choose the most appropriate unit of measure.**
**Write *in., ft., mi., c., qt., pt., gal., oz., lb.,* or *T.***

| | a | b |
|---|---|---|
| **1.** | width of a kitchen table ______ | capacity of a swimming pool ______ |
| **2.** | weight of a bag of potatoes ______ | length of your thumb ______ |

**Circle the best measurement.**

| | a | b |
|---|---|---|
| **3.** | capacity of a baby bottle<br>2 L    200 mL | capacity of a milk carton<br>20 mL    1 L |
| **4.** | distance between your eyes<br>10 cm    25 mm | mass of a notebook<br>100 g    1 kg |

**Change each measurement to the smaller unit.**

| | a | b | c |
|---|---|---|---|
| **5.** | 2 gal. = ______ pt. | 5 kg = ______ g | 3 T. = ______ lb. |

**Change each measurement to the larger unit.**

| | a | b | c |
|---|---|---|---|
| **6.** | 70,000 mm = ______ m | 8 pt. = ______ gal. | 4,000 g = ______ kg |

**Compare. Write <, >, or =.**

| | a | b |
|---|---|---|
| **7.** | 450 cm ______ 45 m | 24 c. ______ 2 qt. |
| **8.** | 4 ft. ______ 50 in. | 1,900 mL ______ 2 L |
| **9.** | 2 mi. ______ 16,000 ft. | 48 km ______ 5,000 m |

**Guess and check to solve each problem.**

**10.** Jane has 43 cents. She has 8 coins. Find the coins and the number of each that Jane has.

Answer ______________________

**11.** The playground director has a total of 24 basketballs and footballs. He has 6 more footballs than basketballs. How many of each does he have?

Answer ______________________

**12.** Jeremy stores his baseball cards in two boxes. He has 36 cards altogether. If one box holds twice as many cards as the other, how many cards are in each box?

Answer ______________________

**13.** Caroline and Ron have 11 goldfish in all. Caroline has three more than Ron. How many fish do they each have?

Answer ______________________

**14.** The ostrich and the emu are the two largest birds. An emu is usually $\frac{1}{2}$ the size of an ostrich. The sum of their heights is 150 inches. How tall is the average ostrich?

Answer ______________________

## Angles

A **ray** is an endless straight path starting at one point.

**Say: ray BG**

**Write: $\overrightarrow{BG}$**

An **angle** is two rays with a common endpoint.

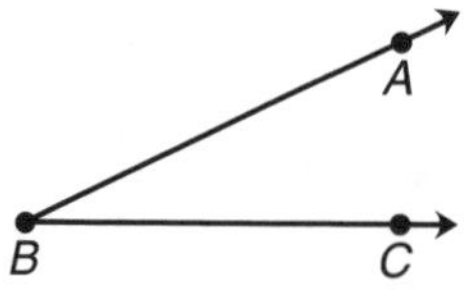


**Say: angle ABC or angle CBA**

**Write: ∠ABC or ∠CBA or ∠B**

**Angles are measured in *degrees* (°).**

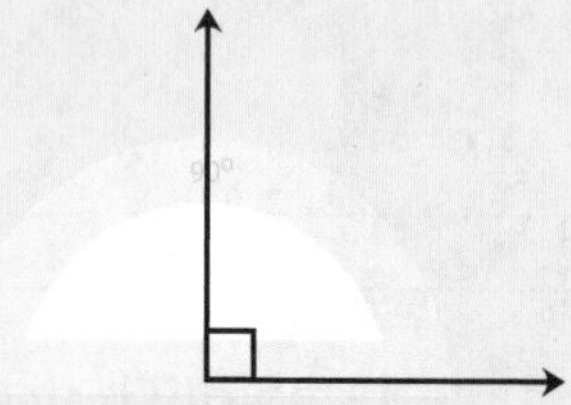

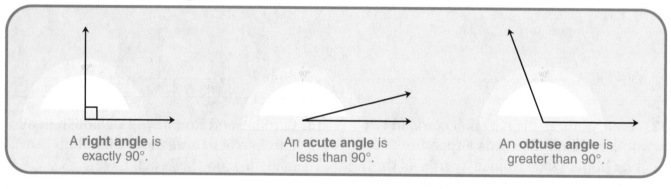

A **right angle** is exactly 90°.

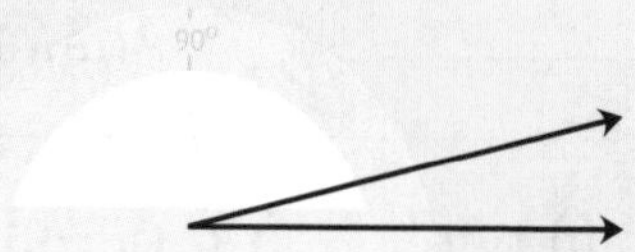

An **acute angle** is less than 90°.

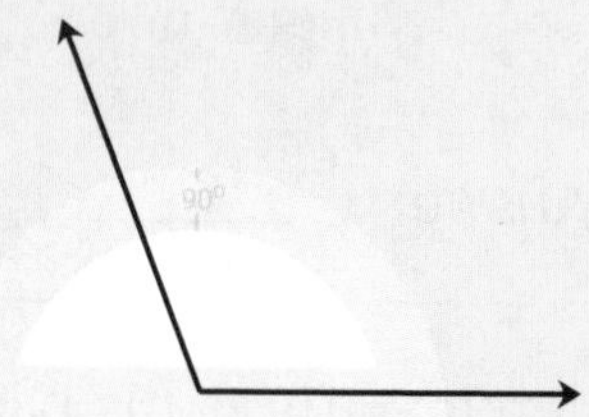

An **obtuse angle** is greater than 90°.

**Name each angle using symbols.**

| | a | b | c | d |
|---|---|---|---|---|
| **1.** | 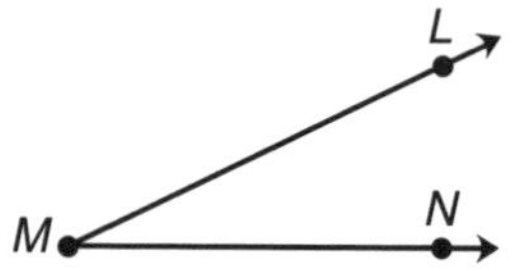  | 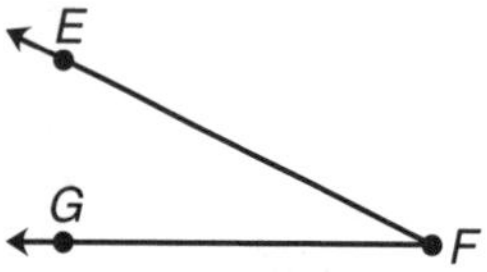  | 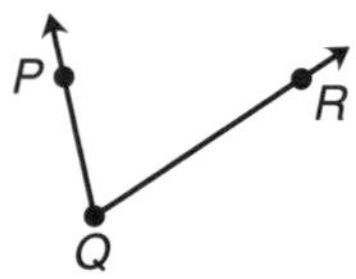  | 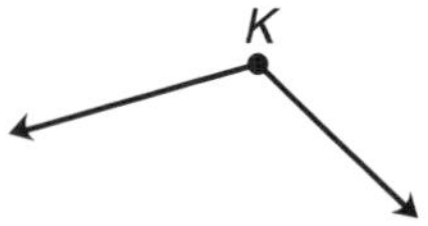  |
| | ∠LMN or ∠NML or ∠M | ________ | ________ | ________ |

**Name each angle. Write *right angle, acute angle,* or *obtuse angle.***

| | a | b | c | d |
|---|---|---|---|---|
| **2.** | 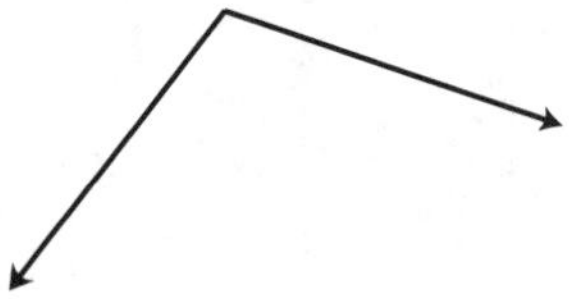 |  | 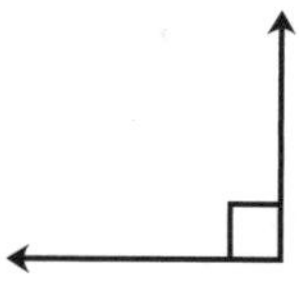 | 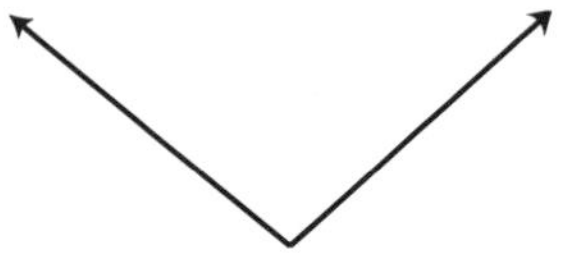 |
| | obtuse angle | ________ | ________ | ________ |

# Perimeter

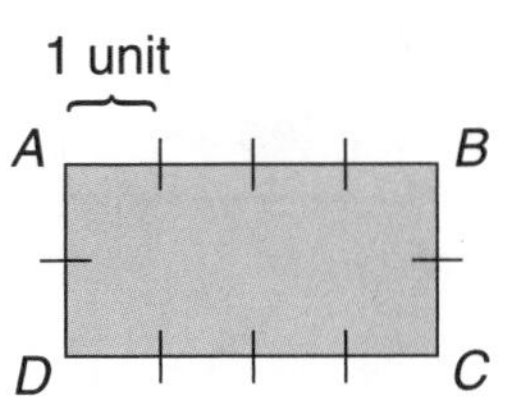


**Perimeter** is the distance around a figure.

To find the perimeter of a figure, count the number of units around the figure.

Find the perimeter of this rectangle by counting units.

Start at point A. Move clockwise and count the units from A to B (4), to C (6), to D (10), to A (12).

The perimeter of this rectangle is 12 units.

**Find the perimeter of each rectangle.**

| | a | b | c |
|---|---|---|---|
| **1.** | 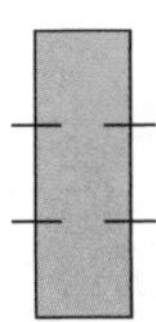 8 units | 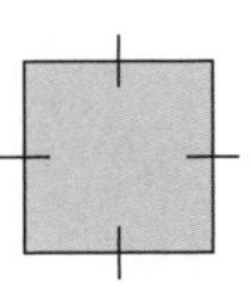 ________ | 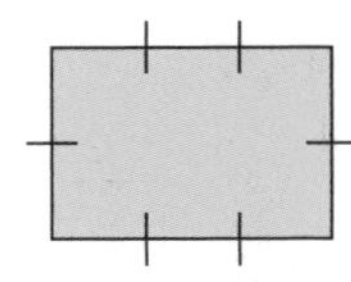 ________ |
| **2.** | 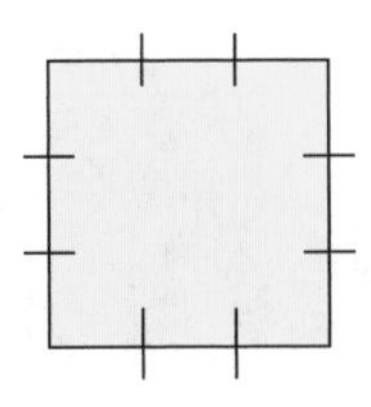 ________ | ________ | 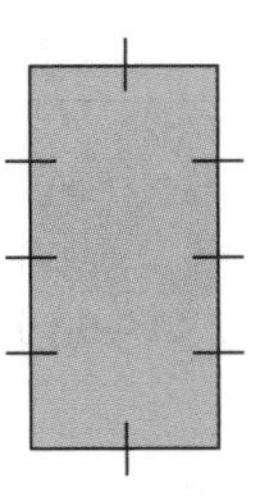 ________ |
| **3.** | 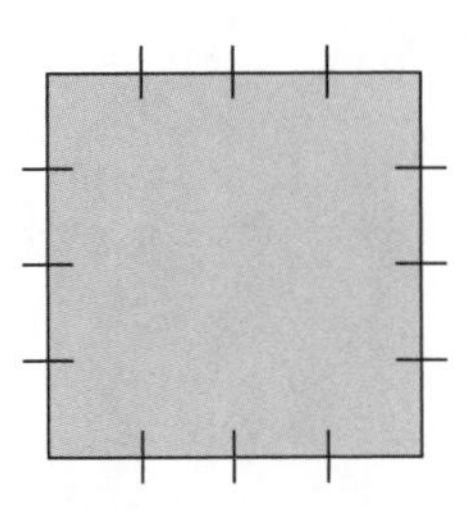 ________ | 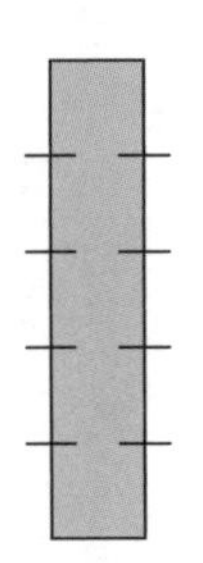 ________ | 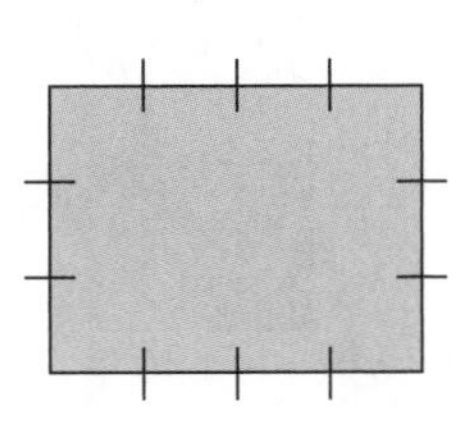 ________ |

# Formula for Perimeter of a Rectangle

To find the perimeter of a rectangle, you can also use a **formula.**

**Rectangles**

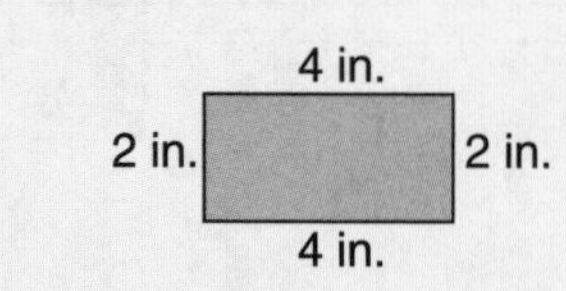


$\boldsymbol{P = \text{side } 1 + \text{side } 2 + \text{side } 3 + \text{side } 4}$

$P = 4 + 2 + 4 + 2$

$P = 12$ in.

**Squares (rectangles with four equal sides)**

Since the sides of a square are equal,

$\boldsymbol{P = 4 \times \text{any side}}$

$P = 4 \times 2 = 8$ cm

**Find the perimeter of each figure by using one of the formulas.**

*a* *b*

**1.**

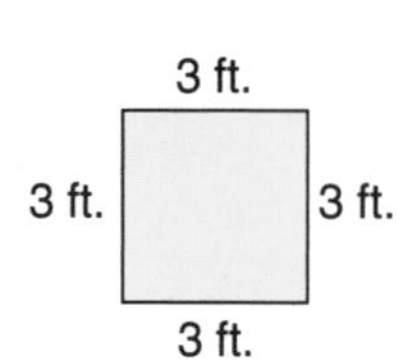


12 feet

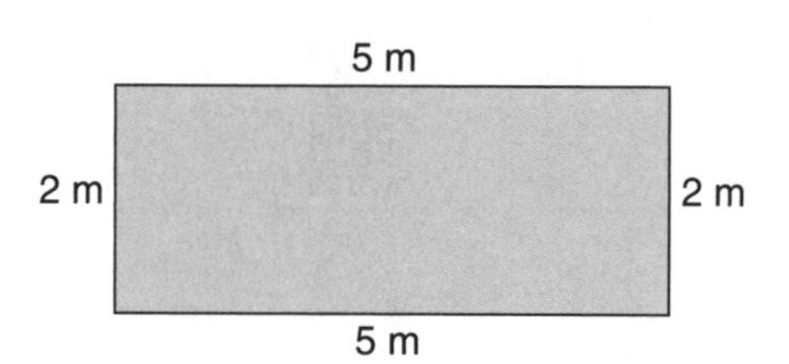


**2.**

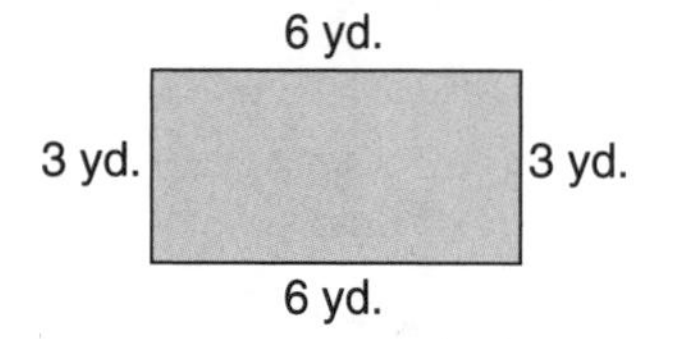


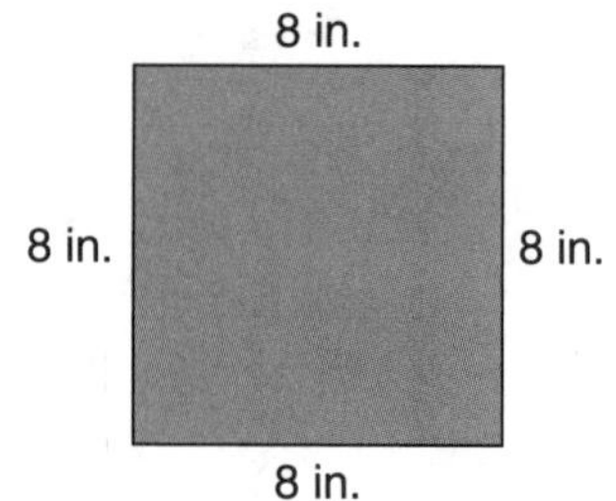


**3.**

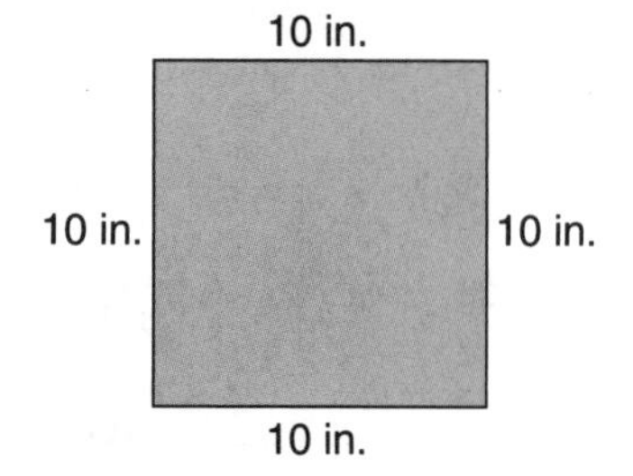


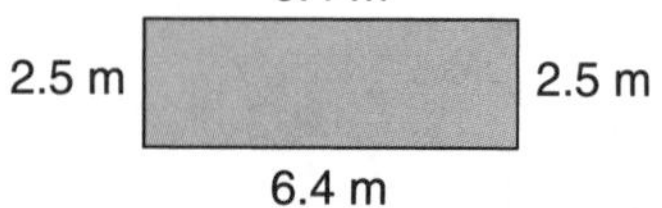

# Area

The **area** of a figure is the number of square units that cover its surface.

This is 1 square unit.

Count the number of square units to find the area of a figure.

The area of this figure is 8 square units.

**Find the area of each figure.**

| | a | b |
|---|---|---|
| 1. | 5 square units | ______ |
| 2. | ______ | ______ |
| 3. | ______ | ______ |

# Formula for Area of a Rectangle

To find the area of a rectangle, you can also use a formula.

The formula, **A = l × w,** means the area of a rectangle equals the length times the width.

**Remember, write your answer in *square* units.**

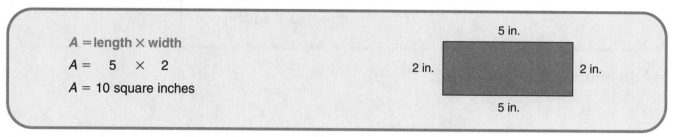


**Find the area of each rectangle by using the formula.**

*a* | *b*

**1.**

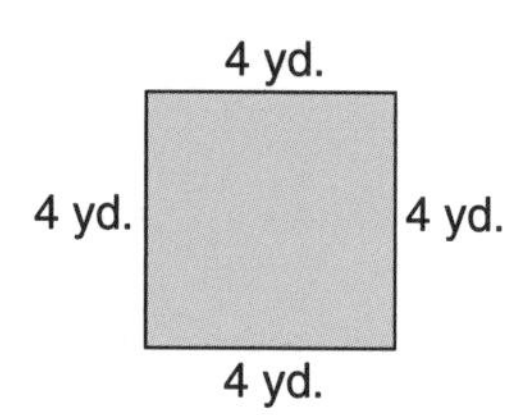


16 square yards ______

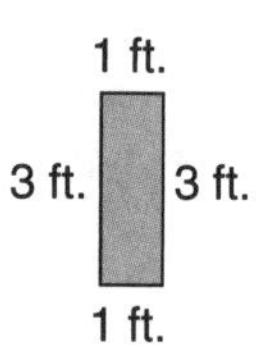


______

**2.**

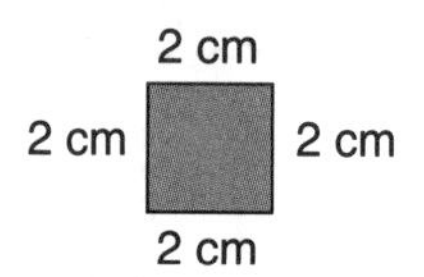


______

6 in.
2 in. 2 in.
6 in.

______

**3.**

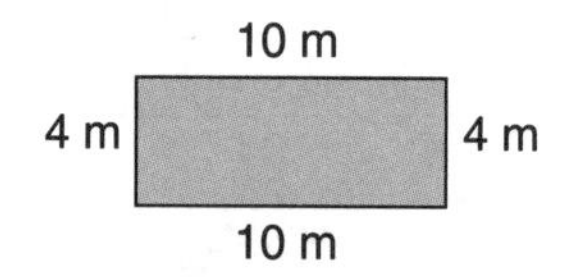


______

12 mm
12 mm 12 mm
12 mm

______

## Problem-Solving Method: Use a Formula

Carla needs to replace the pad covering her dining room table. Her table is 7 feet long and 4 feet wide. How much padding does she need?

**Understand the problem.**

- **What do you want to know?**
  how much padding Carla needs to cover her table

- **What information do you know?**
  The tabletop is 7 feet long and 4 feet wide.
  The table is a rectangle.

**Plan how to solve it.**

- **What method can you use?**
  You can use a formula.

**Solve it.**

- **How can you use this method to solve the problem?**
  Since you want to know how much material will cover the surface of the table, you can use the formula for the area of a rectangle.

$$A = l \times w$$
$$A = 7 \times 4$$
$$A = 28$$

- **What is the answer?**
  Carla needs 28 square feet of padding.

**Look back and check your answer.**

- **Is your answer reasonable?**
  You can check by drawing the top of the table and dividing it into square units. Then count the units.

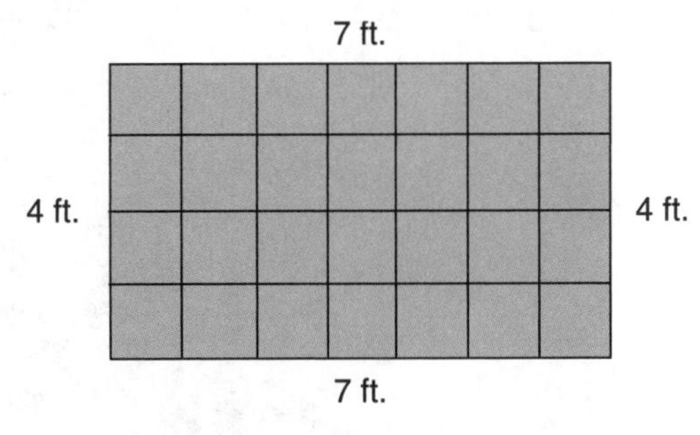


There are 28 squares.
The answer is reasonable.

**Use a formula for area or perimeter to solve each problem.**

1. Sam wants to put a fence around his garden. The garden is 6 yards long and 4 yards wide. How many yards of fencing should he order?

Answer ______________________________

2. The floor of Kim's room measures 13 feet in length and 11 feet in width. How many square feet of carpet does she need to cover her floor?

Answer ______________________________

3. Emily wants to put trim around a square window that measures 3 feet on each side. How many feet of trim does she need?

Answer ______________________________

4. One acre is equal to 4,840 square yards. Jamal's backyard is 121 yards long and 40 yards wide. How big is Jamal's backyard in acres?

Answer ______________________________

5. A professional soccer field is 75 meters wide and 110 meters long. If you run all the way around the soccer field, how far do you go?

Answer ______________________________

**Name each angle using symbols.**

**1.**

a

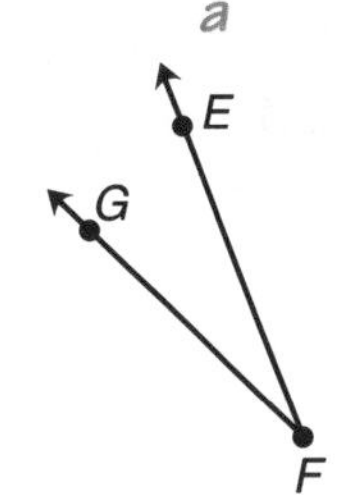


b

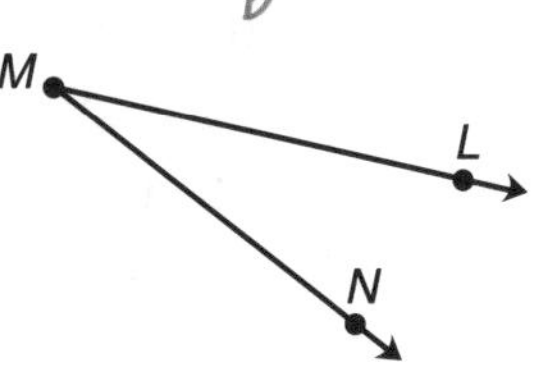


c

B A C

d

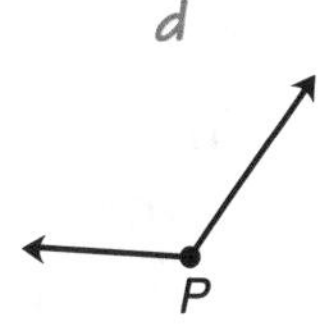


**Name each angle. Write *right angle, acute angle,* or *obtuse angle.***

**2.**

a

b

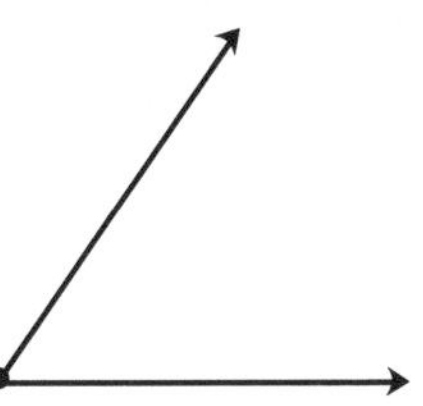

c

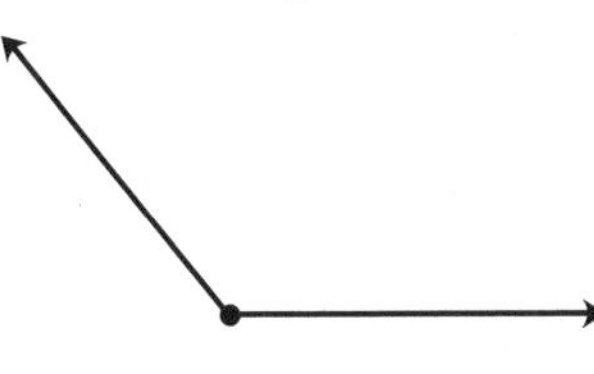

d

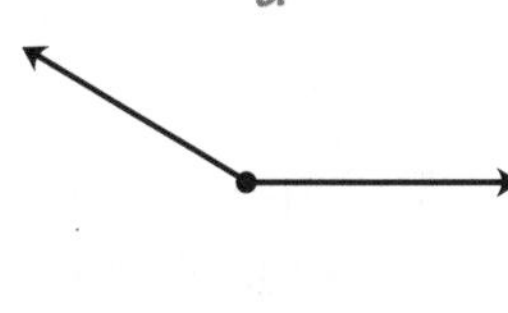

**Find the perimeter of each figure.**

**3.**

a

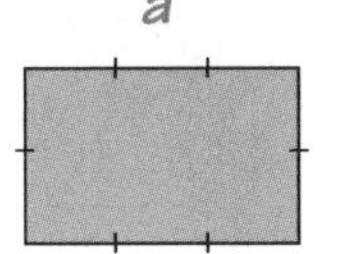

b

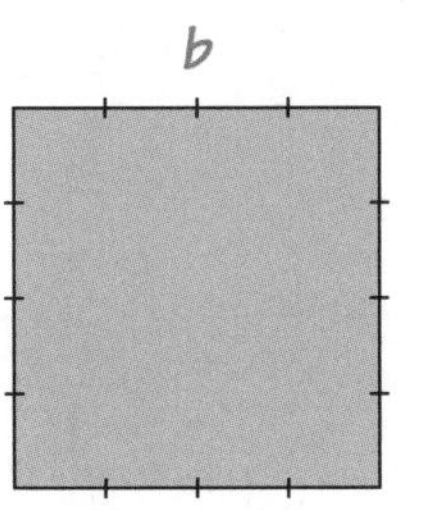

c

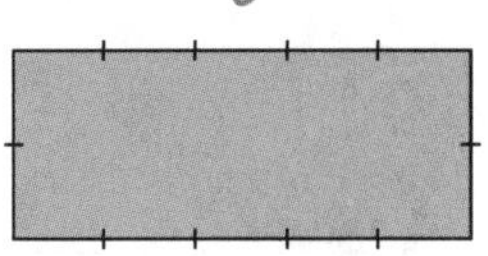

**Find the area of each figure.**

**4.**

a

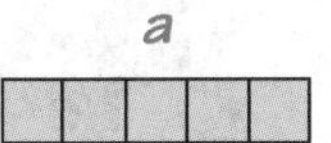

b

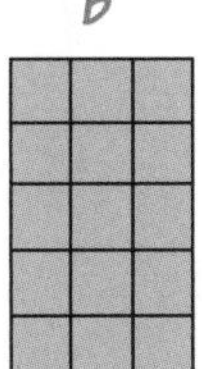

c

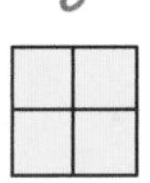

**Use a formula to solve each problem.**

5. The class bulletin board is 4 feet long and 6 feet wide. How many feet of border does Mr. Chow need to surround the bulletin board?

Answer ______________________

6. The school yard is twice as long as it is wide. The width is 23 yards. How much fencing is needed to enclose the school yard?

Answer ______________________

7. The park is 3 miles long and 2 miles wide. Manuel walked around the park two times. How many miles did he walk in all?

Answer ______________________

8. A National Hockey League ice rink is 58 meters long and 26 meters wide. How many square meters of ice cover the rink's surface?

Answer ______________________

9. Andy had wood flooring installed in his living room for $12 a square foot. The room measures 9 feet by 12 feet. What did the wood flooring cost?

Answer ______________________